Labels

Joi Donaldson

Labels
Copyright © 2015 by Joi Donaldson

Get social with me!
Facebook: Right Side Reign, LLC
Twitter: Elemental_Jah
Instagram: Personal: I_The_Abstract /Photography: RightSideReignRVA
Blog: stackedpoetpages.tumblr.com
Photo Site: 500px.com/JoiUnspeakable

Acknowledgement

Additional Photo Credit: Janay
Hargrove & Chy Patterson

Printed in United States of America

10 9 8 7 6 5 4 3 2 1

ISBN: 978-1507528846

Catty. Bitchy. Petty.
Natural. Relaxed. Weave.
Dark. Light. Bitter. Angry

I meet women every day who are fighting with what to call themselves. I meet myself in the mirror every morning and do the same. We wonder who and what we are. We try to keep it light and own up to one sense of being - a writer, make-up artist, designer, mechanic - but in reality we are so much more. I believe it scares women to say they are more than one noun: that we are more than just mothers, lawyers, physicists, artists. That we own the multitasking copyrights. Yet we allow the world to label us for going after multiple dreams as overachievers, scatterbrained, selfish, busybodies. Why can't we be everything we are made up to be?

On the flip side, at times we take on too much. We shoulder responsibilities we weren't asked to uphold. Overcoming what our parents called or didn't call us, an ex-lover's scathing last words, what society dictates we are supposed to be. We carry on the strong stereotype of having it all together, when many of us are dying inside. Or worse - have died because we didn't let anyone know we were hurting. Because we aren't allowed sweat to even form, let alone be seen.

Most of us have forgotten how to be human.

To fall short.

To say no.

And because of that, we've incurred the labels of bitch, an angry black woman, bossy, hardheaded, stubborn.

Our men – ourselves - have cast these labels upon us and we have taken up the banners and held them proudly. But at what cost? What about the healing?

Who has time for it, right?

We do.

I don't want women to think that loving, supporting, complimenting each other is this impossible mindset to reach. It's incredibly possible. When you see a beautiful sista, tell her she's beautiful. It may be the first time she's heard it genuinely in years. If you like her shoes, bag, make-up, nails, hair, cheekbones, the way she holds her head - tell her. We've waged war on each other long enough. It's time to heal each other from within. And it starts with stopping the hate. It starts with being a part of our own rescue.

Can We Win?
If we ask for too much attention
We're thirsty
If we ask for too little
We're suspicious
If we open our legs too wide
We're whores
If we close them too tightly
We're prudes
If we're in the club
We're basic
If we're out the club
We're "too good"
If I say I'm powerful
I'm overstepping
If I don't say anything
I'm weak
I'm asking you
When can we win?

Some of the stories in this book are hard to read. They may trigger some long-repressed emotions to come to the surface. While reading this, you may cry, get angry, cheer, clap for those who made it to the other side of healthy and mourn for those who didn't. If any of those well up within you, this book, these women and their stories, poetry, art and testimonies have done their job.

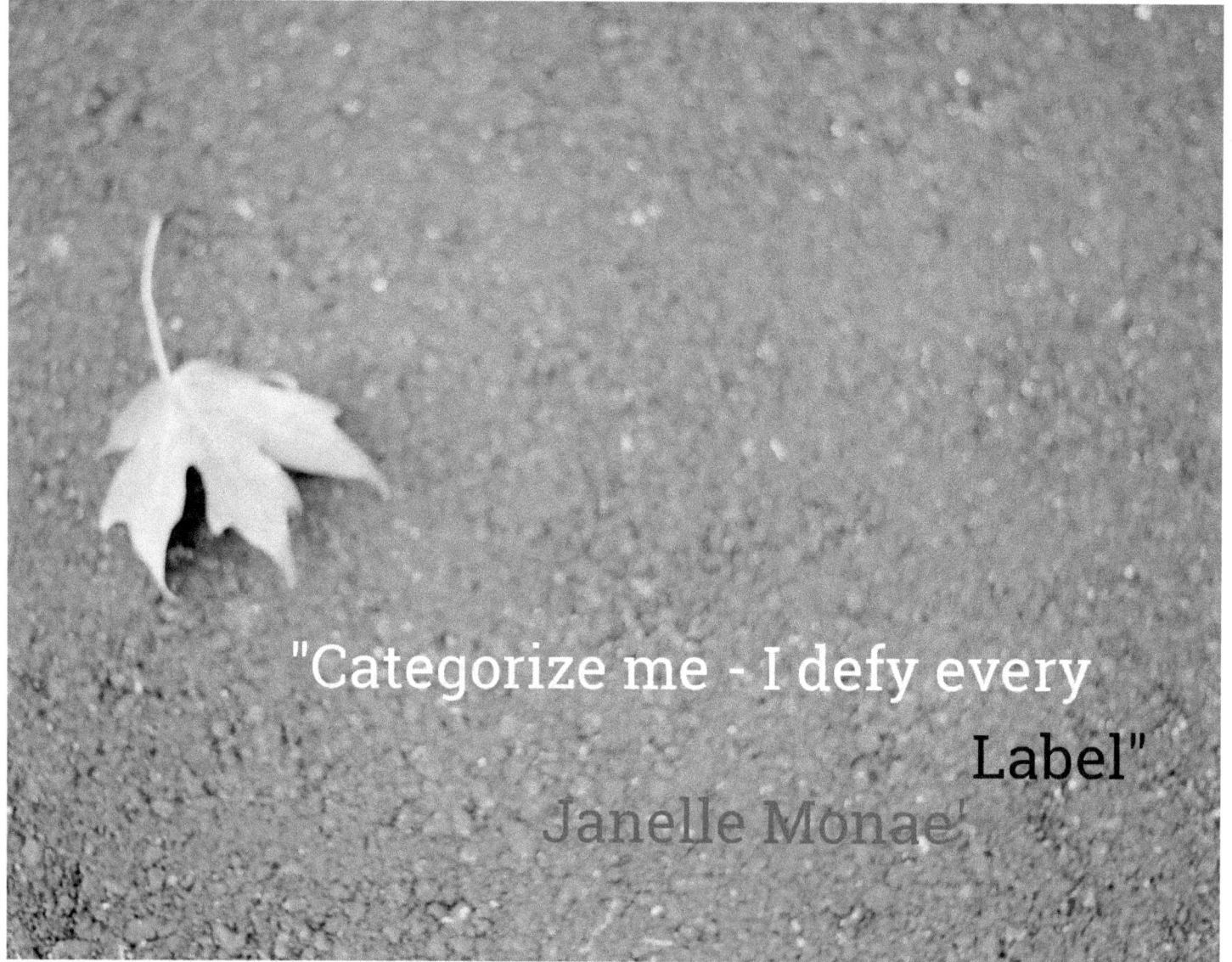

"Categorize me - I defy every Label"

Janelle Monae"

Latasha Johnson
Teshawn Butler
Brandy Bower
Queen Johnson
Deidra Stevenson
Verandah-Maureen
B. Ross
Janay Hargrove
Jessica Snyder
Andrea Nicole
Christina White
Nudasha Gratic-Fludd
Nickey McMullen
Dominique Henry
Maruim Eltahir
Matisha Williams
Monica Bailey

Thank you all for being so vulnerable. I pray whoever's reading your story finds strength.

To flip over the tags and write our own definitions.

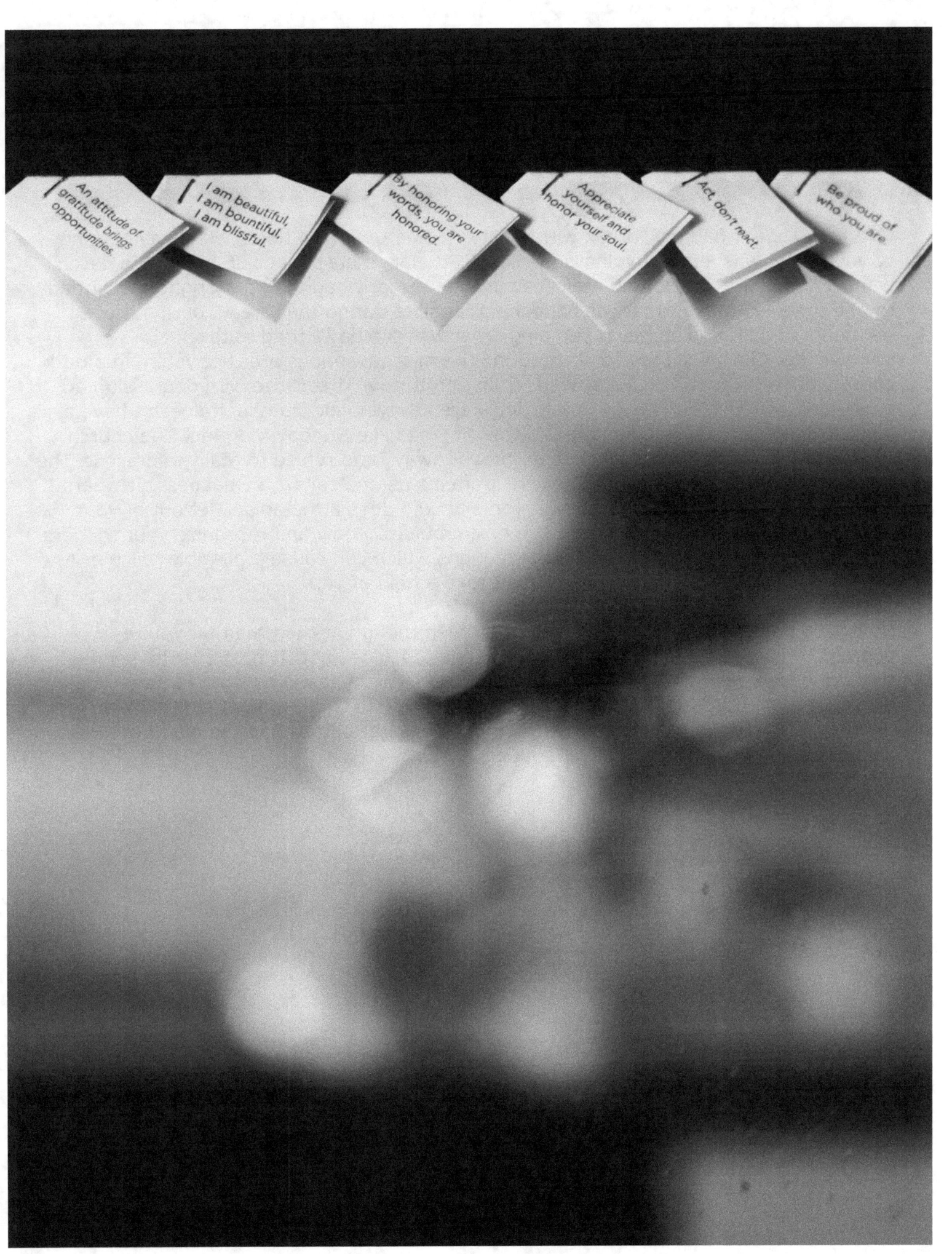

Five years ago, I had my "break with reality". Being up for 24 hours will do something to you. But it was either a voluntarily trip to St. Mary's hospital or 36 hours in a psych ward. I chose St. Mary's. And their food was amazing. I had to find a bright spot. I had to find a way to make what was happening tangible during that break, during those moments of guilt and stomach pumping. That was the day I tried to take my own life. Clinical depression is not fun. The misconceptions are that you're in a dark corner with a blanket over your head, crying profusely. That those with depression are constantly negative and believe that things are always bad. Truth is, it doesn't have a look. It looks normal. It looks put-together. It looks like Sunday morning. The church community that tries to insist you can "pray it away" and refuse to really address it. The black community that refuses to believe it affects us and calls it a weakness. It wears the shade of denial quite well. Prayer works and so does a therapist. Get out of your pride and admit that you have an issue or a problem. Know and recognize your triggers and limitations. Excuse yourself from situations which can cause a possible tailspin. Ask for help to get a handle on it so it doesn't take a hold of you.

Suicide is one of the most selfish acts ever, even though at the time that you're contemplating it, you think that it's going to help. It does not. It destroys the people that you leave behind. I don't think I've ever seen my husband as worried and distraught and upset as when he had to take his wife to the ER to get her stomach pumped. I would not wish that on anybody. It does get better. And I'm glad I'm here. Diagnosis – I'm okay….and I have fabulous shoes.
Life is grand.

- Latasha White Johnson

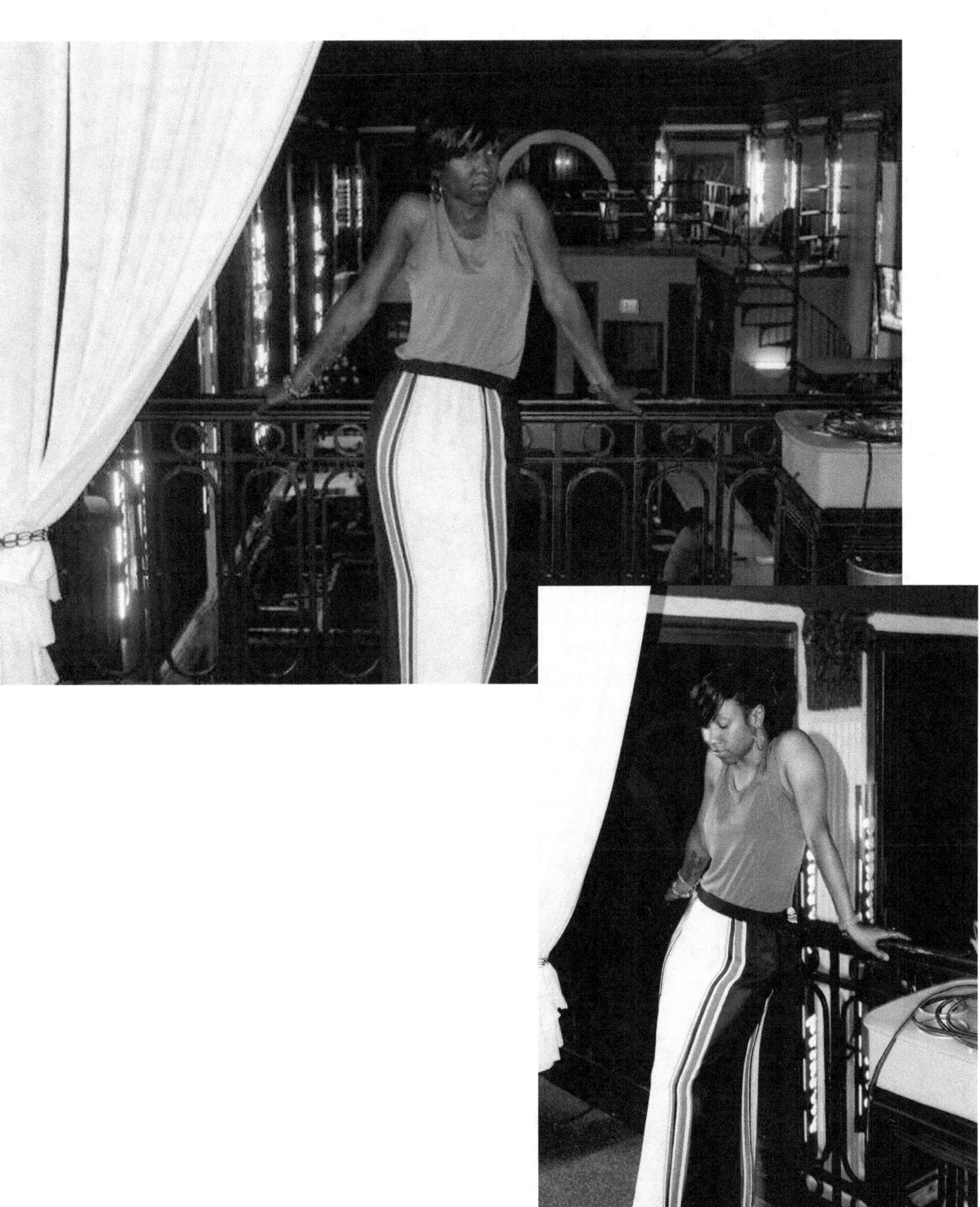

Dear God

Help me
It's Your daughter
and I'm tired
Physically. Emotionally. Lovingly. Achingly. Tired.
I'm spent
with no words left
I keep falling with nowhere to land
my face is open and life keeps hitting more square
and I'm tired.
My fuel is low.
I'm empty.
Dear Lord it's me
I'm here
and I'm tired.

Capes

Those days when I just want to fall apart
much rather lay in the dirt cascading down my garden of pity
I want to scream
I need to scream for sanctuary
an SOS for help as I drown with my life vest tied tight
why can't you rescue me?
I plead the fifth in my own defense and relinquish my right to sanity
I'm tired
I'm lonely
this thankless job for mine
I just want to be held
want to be comforted as I muffle my cries in your shoulder and clench my fist across your chest
the chest opposite yours my insignia rests
I'm the hero in need of rescue
with my cape caught on my heels
when will it be safe to let the mask fall?

My Orientation is

Authentic

Unapologetic

Unwavering

Not a Phase

Bucking the Norm

Refusing Hate

Accepting Love

Epic

I don't
have
to be
what you want
me to be

Said Peace

I'm not going to overthink this
Today
I am at peace
And said peace
Is worth more than the gold placed
on my fingers
The bags dropped in my lap
The waters riding up my thighs as I
wade in this sea of peace
Amounts to more than words can
say
It's passionate
Hungry
Heavy and satiated
This swelling, quickening echo of
peace
has overcome me
And I have no beckoning words
It's just taken me over
And I just glow

I tried to think of what others have labeled me - talented, creative - that
puts pressure on me. It leads me to be fearful of failing.
I'm a perfectionist. I heard a quote that said, "where the perfectionist is
present, fear is usually in the passenger seat." That is so true for me.
But I've even labeled myself scared, and it keeps me from pursuing things.

I am scared I couldn't have kids. Along came Noah. Scared I was gonna lose
Josiah and he's still here.
I'm taking this as a chance to face my fears.
Little by little I'm overcoming, and it feels good.

- Deidra Stevenson

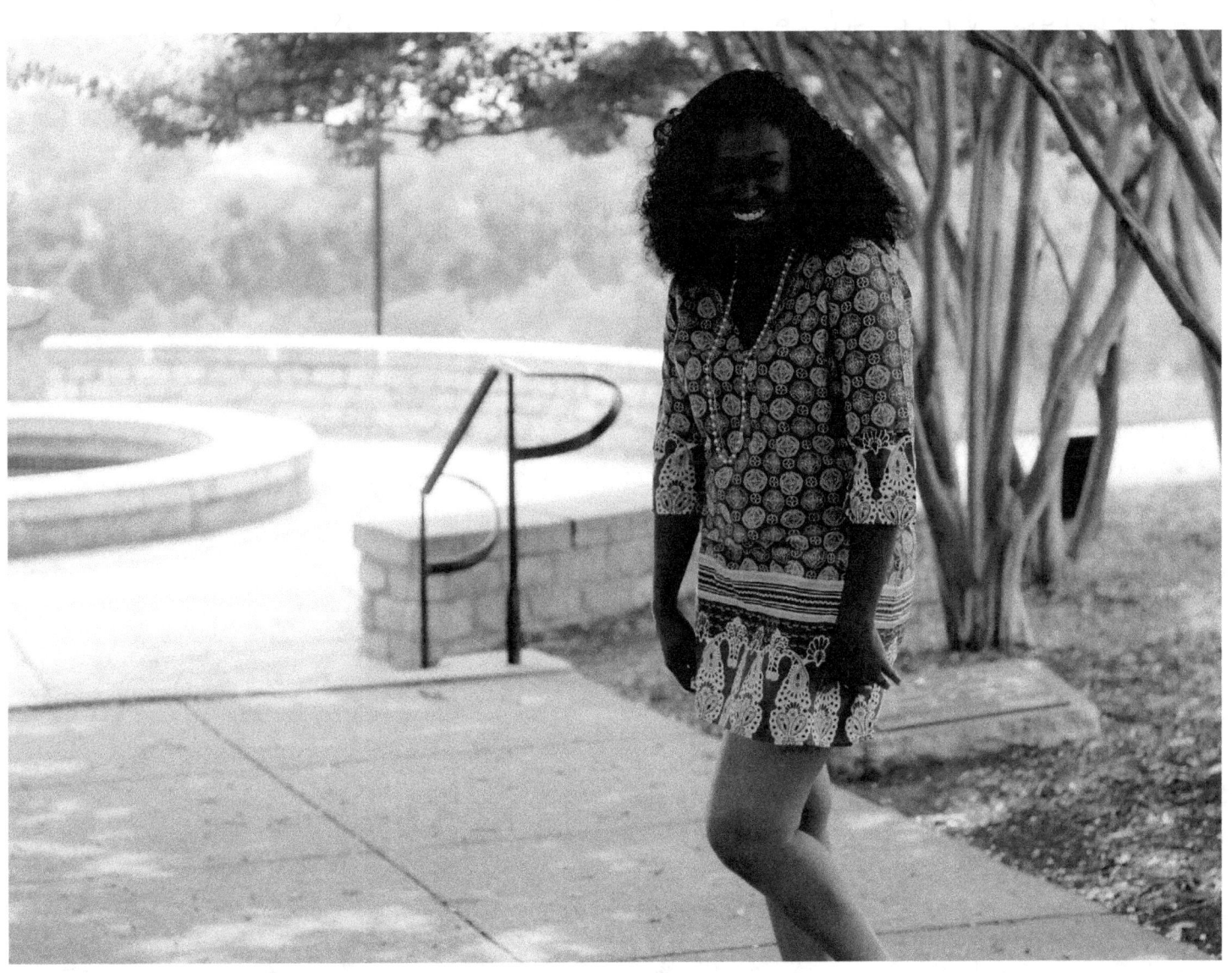

Black Sheep: A Whiny History Lesson

Cue the predictable.
Cue the, "what are you?"
"Are you biracial?"
"What are your people?"
Im too uncomfortable to ask my real questions,
like…
"why are you so…
white?
Why by sight don't you match the normal conventions.
Or the stereotypical connections made when I see you?
Ah,
you must be the "black sheep" of your people.
No pun intended."
No,
I'm not offended,
just really…
worried.
I find it funny that things have been assigned a race--
A man made falsity in the first place
but my friends identify the white music from the black,
and the right attitudes from those that
epitomize color.
It's sadly just another way to perpetuate the issue.
To further classify a people that all came from the same place.
Whom at some point had the same face until migratory factors kicked in.
Before noted differences in skin,
and in phenotype.
Yea, that's right:
The snow bunnies weren't always white
—they just stayed long enough away from sun,
and only then did they become pearled beauties.
I don't know what it means to
talk Black.
I just know that
conversate
AIN'T
a word.
Yet artists have the audacity,
the nerve
to put it in song.
Great.
Now the world can sing along to what they think is Black vernacular.
That's just spectacular,
more global citizens to correct along the way.
And can someone please explain the difference between
the letter A and the letter R?

Apparently,
A is for affection,
R suggests we've come far,
you get it my Niggar--
the new way to be pleasantly oppressive.
I'm not a sellout because I value the promise of a good education.
I'm a sellout if I buy into my people's damnation and I'll be damned if my kids
won't know that.
I don't know what it means to
look Black,
but I know that I don't resemble that of an Oreo.
Can you dip me in milk and eat me?
No.
Get your minds out the gutter…
Wrap it around me being just another
female to be respected,
another sister to be protected.
Those are my reparations right there.
And in case I wasn't clear,
don't ask me what I am
—the who is more important.
The question will only shorten my patience and increase my sarcasm.
There are people
—and you can ask 'em
what kinds of things I've said when asked,
"Hey, what are you?"

…"Human"

- Verandah-Maureen

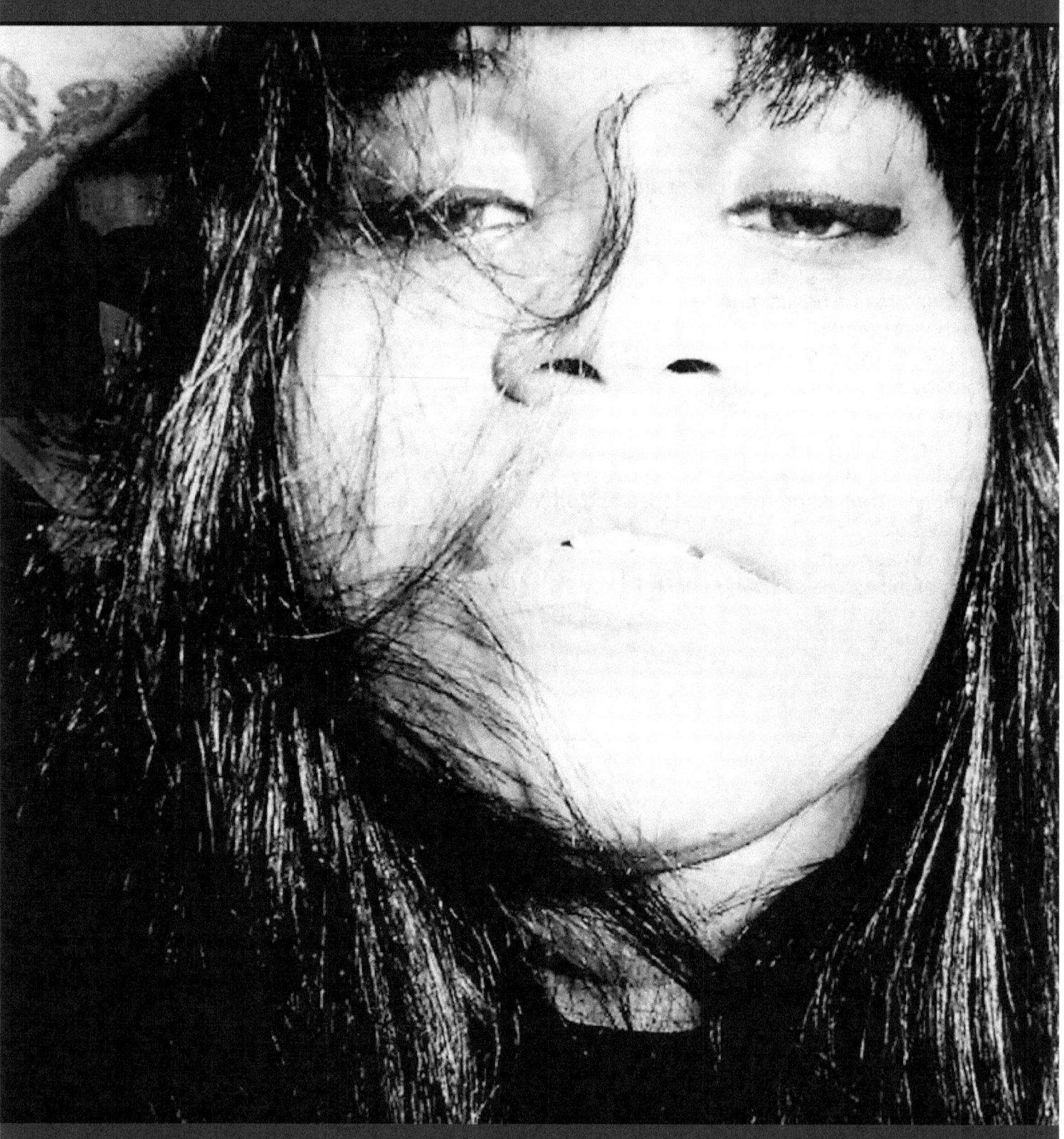

If I write about you
You either are given life or death in my pages
You've given life or caused death in my life
So to live and die by the pen
Is a stance I go to war for
Every day
My weapons line the bottom of my bag, itching to touch straight blue lines
To write about you
About me
About this world
The ups and downs and constant left turns
If I write about you
Me

To Believe In Me

Where do I belong?
Where do I begin
I belong to the earth and the moon
The stars and the ships
The waves and all energy
I get lost sometimes
Forget my name and all sense of direction
I lose sight and make rash decisions
Trying to get back to normal
Where my hair's everywhere
And I feel the most free
Believe in me
When I don't make sense
Which is often the case
Believe in the life I lead if only in my head
If only I'm the one knowing the truth
Believe in me
Once and in all things

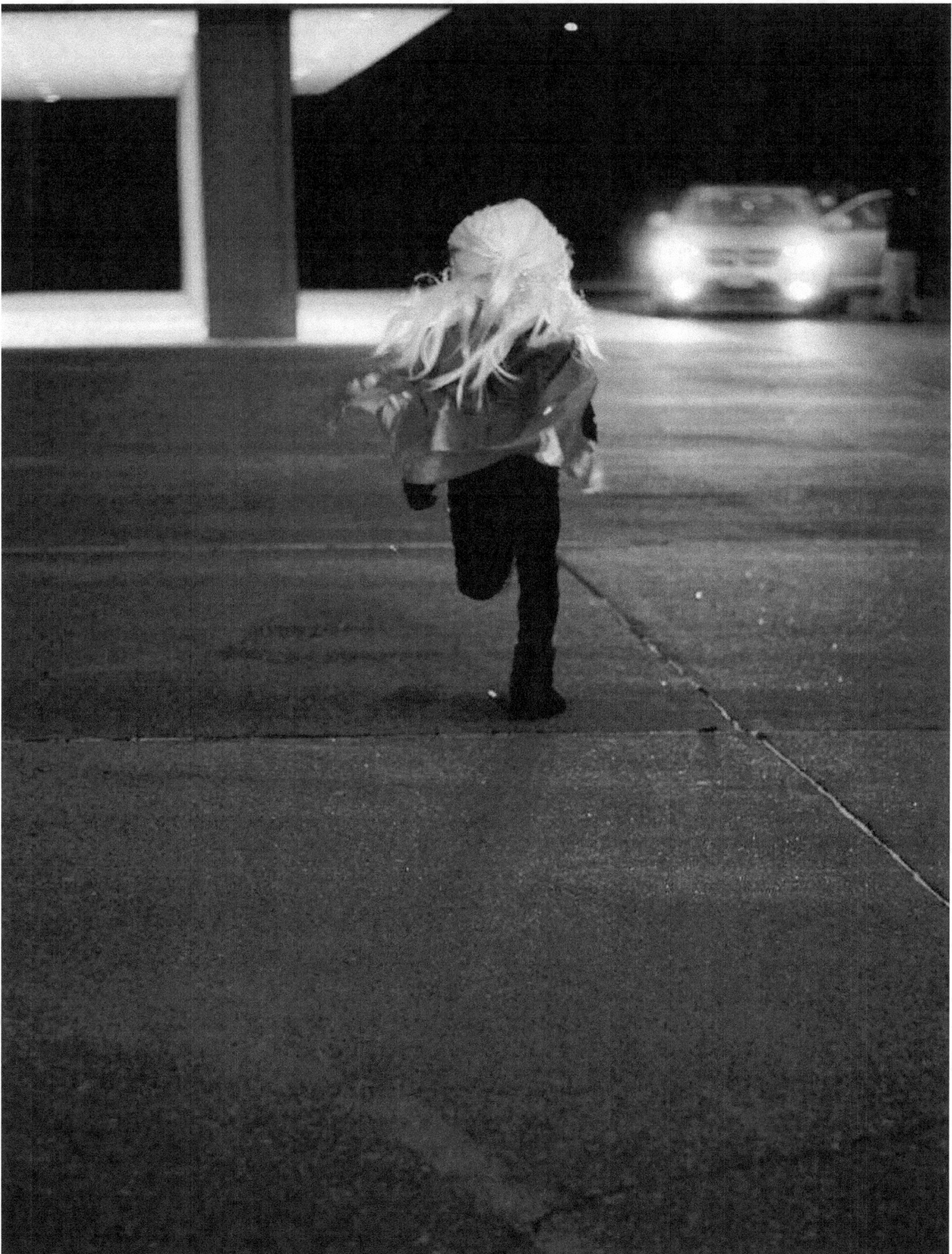

Existing While Female

Long ago, he told me he'd spread rumors if I didn't have sex with him.
Me.
The 14 year old freshman who hadn't a clue about anything and everything.
He called my house
He harassed me in the hallways
Paraded other girls in front of me that shot daggers my way
Yet still
I should feel "thankful" for this much attention from an upperclassman
I must have done something to spark this flame
When all I did was exist in a moment of time
All I did was share my name
Black men
As much as I love you
At times
I avoid you
Sad to say I have to operate in healthy fear
Be wise of my surroundings and be weary of anyone who comes near
In dark corners
Around the aisle
In a crowd because I can't defend myself
Because to be felt up and humiliated by someone who looks like you...
To be alone with the possibilities of what could've happened
If I reacted
How can I run to the arms of a man who called me a bitch because a rapper told him to?
You're killing my once strong belief in you
You pull us apart and chastise our hair, dress, authenticity
Yet you're pissed when we decline your advances
A black woman has become a downgrade to the masses
Yet we are told to understand your struggle
This isn't our lesson to teach
We can pass fault all day but ultimately it's the children we need to reach
Those who will grow up defending and be mending of a woman
And not another generation to laugh at her rape and be undercutting
Of her shade
Her temper
We are angry because we have nowhere to turn
To be alone and cautious is mostly what we've learned
White man
Fox News says it's my attire
Why does it matter?
Did a high hemline really spark a fire?
To say I'm asking for something a man should've taught another to withhold
A woman is not a dumping ground regardless of what you've been told
How I dress is my preference
No man's right to rescind

Because you don't know how it feels
And those men who do remain silent
And the most vicious cycle begins again
A black woman's privilege in turn doesn't add up to shit
On either side
Yet still I try
To live in a man's world
Full of unlawful expectations of a girl
How I have to know 5 getaways just in case
Again, who is here to protect us?
It's just me in this space
Any man
Every man
Your whistles
Free drinks
Business cards
Don't equal a night in your bed.
My thighs.
Didn't invite your touch.
My anything is mine to own.

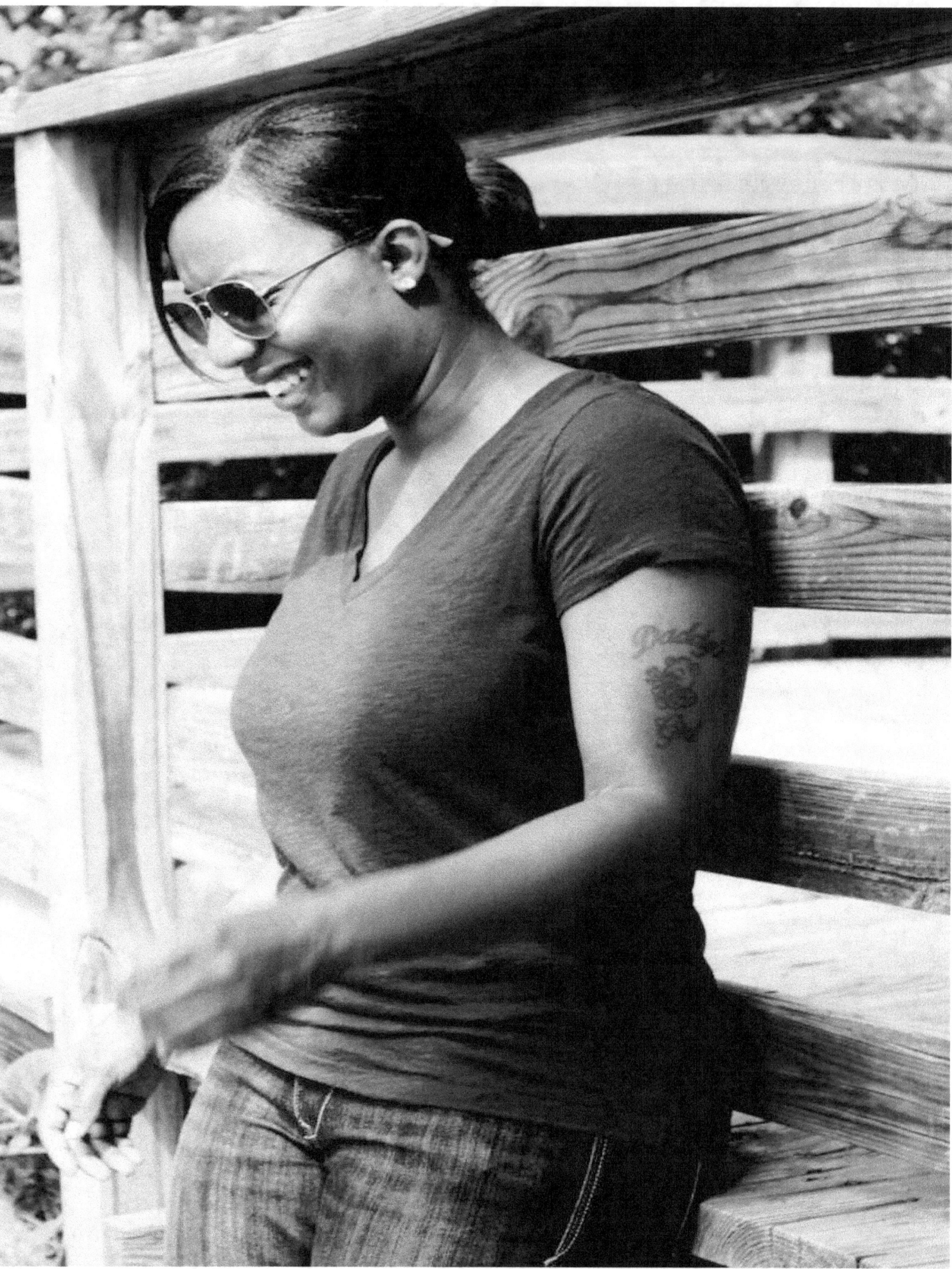

Incompetent. Inefficient. Ineffective. Not really needed.

These are some of the labels thrown at me because of my job. I knew there would be some difficulty in my field, considering it's male-dominant, but I did not know it would come from all angles. My male co-workers don't necessarily see me as an equal. Some may think I've been hired just to reach a quota. I've even heard my Lt say "law enforcement isn't a place for women and there is no room for empathy in law enforcement." Then there are the random men I encounter. I remember having a conversation with a man, and he said to me, "oh, so you're one of *those* women". I replied for him to please explain. He thought that the only reason I got into law enforcement was so I could feed off the power the uniform gives. He thought I was "power tripping". He felt that the only way I was going to get respect from people was to abuse my power by hiding behind the color of blue.

Little does he know, that's totally wrong. I get hit harder and disrespected way more than my male co-workers simply because I'm a female. This uniform doesn't come with automatic compliance from people. It comes with questioning of my authority,
smart remarks, and straight defiance.
I entered this field because I wanted a challenge. I wanted a job that was fulfilling and rewarding. Not so I could run around and be a bitch to people. I'm not an egotistical person and I'm not a "power tripper". I don't abuse my powers to make up for hidden insecurities like men think I do. I'm just trying to live and get a check.

- Brandy Bower

Ladies...
Our light means more than the gossip we spill
The looks that kill
And the hugs that feel
A little bit condescending
Long ago, I stopped pretending
To be okay w/ the naysaying
Overdosed on estrogen and petty conversations
That were baseless and caused division
My mind isn't where you are
But I am you
So where do we go from here?

Sistas...
My mane isn't the same
As yours
Does that mean I'm to be abhorred
Or viewed in a different state of being
Because I tend to cling to what's freeing
For me
And not what sista so-and-so told on YouTube
Why does it matter?
My attitude
These 16 shades of black we own
Whether it's a weave or the locks that sprout from her dome are her
own

Chicks...
If one more complains about a
dark-skinned
light-skinned
Entrepreneurial
Age
Sexist
Illegitimate twerkdown
competition..
I'm on a mission
To unify but not pacify
This cataclysmic condition we sit ourselves in
Calling each other names and demeaning our own presence
Starting and continuing beef where there is none
The essence of us we continue to defame
All because she didn't speak
Maybe it's because she doesn't know your name

Or the look on your face says it's all game
A means to an end
Yet we punish our own earths
Yall, we need to mend
We, women, are the earth from which the sun
Sons
Spin
The self, right and left-hate

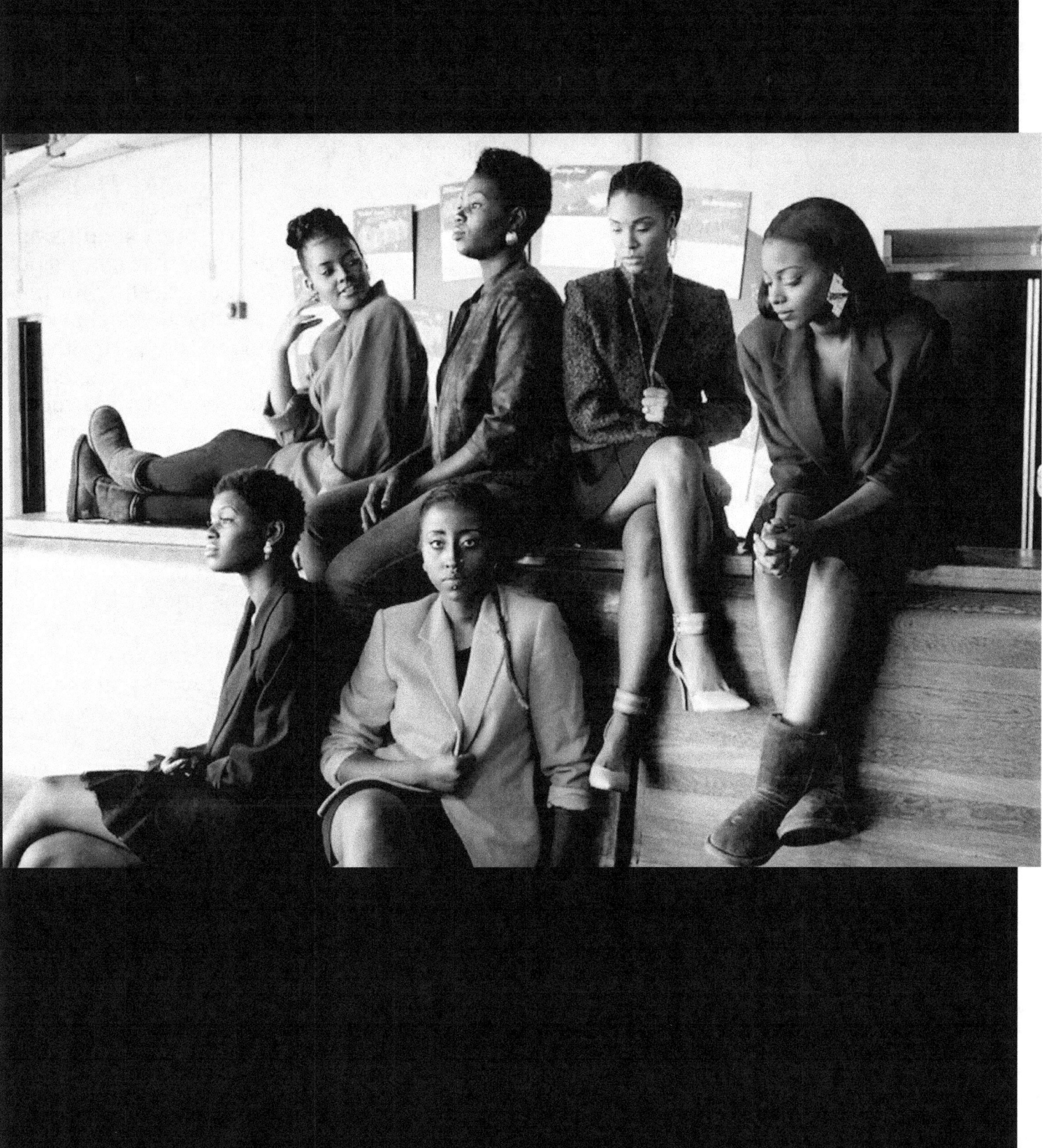

Some Men/Most Women

"You look like you're gaining some weight.
Are you stressed?"
Let's see:
In building dynasties without the S on my chest
I get weary.
Things slip my mind.
But I keep rising.
A little jiggle here and there isn't that surprising.
But I get healthy for me.
Not to suit your ideal or plus
Unless you're shooting in the gym with me
Kindly shut the eff up
"I hate those head wraps. Hair bonnets and such."
Honestly I don't understand why you care so much.
Can't wear weave but God forbid a few rollers
And more and more it's your chauvinistic attitude I'm over
My crown gets rusty
It takes time to reset these curls
Most days I feel regal and want to show I'm out of this world
But if all you can see are the bonnets and not me under all this fluff
Please, for all intents and purposes, shut the hell up
"You don't do for me like you used to"
Again, let me see
I have mouths to feed and kingdoms to reign and all you do is
teethe
On yesterday when I was just a bluff
But now I see my worth and I have had enough
So please go and leave
And do your best to trust
You'll find that one with no standards, goals or backbone
And you will for good shut the fuck up

Can I talk to you for a little while?
In the mirror
I have to tell myself I love you every day.
It gets easier
But I still forget
Still regret to remember
Until my spirit breaks and I'm looking for the
hole to patch
As I break through the mirror
I shatter the glass, cutting myself on shards of
self-reflection
Emergencies spill down my arms realizing
I haven't fallen too deep down the rabbit hole
Every morning I peak into your bedroom and
remember the anger from yesterday
Why I hold on to that and not you
Scares me
Worries me
As hard as I fought to have you
Being a single mother wasn't in the plans
It's not your fault
I'm fighting generational demons
from your breath every time
I look in your eyes
Dear mirror
Dear child

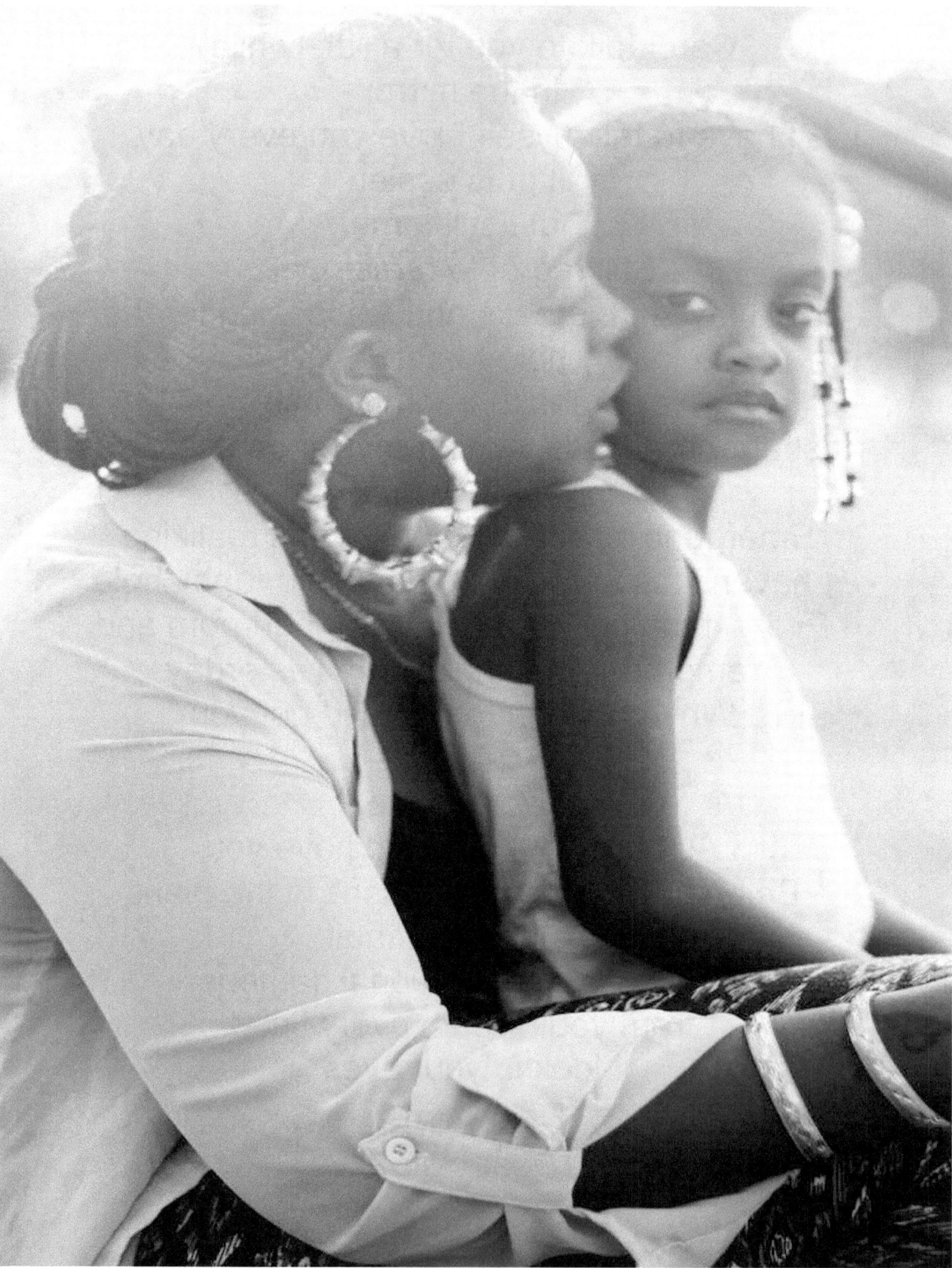

Single mother? I just became a statistic but what does that mean? in my wildest dreams, I never imagined this would be me. Nineteen, round-bellied, stressing and second guessing if I can even handle this. If I could turn back time, I can't say I'd do it again. Maybe then I'd avoid the tears, decrease my fears and live a life more meaningful. Maybe the questions of "where's daddy" would be answerable. Maybe insecurity wouldn't have taken over and I just wanted to feel "complete". How selfish of me to immaturely bring you into the world when a piece of the puzzle was missing. I could have squeamishly laid down, been put to sleep and awakened to just me - but then where would I be? Because even as a single mother: battered, torn, and struggling, I've found myself. I've found that reason for breathing, found something to believe in, found that better half to make me laugh and love unconditionally. I may not have the latest fashion or be a size 6, but I cherish every moment as mother. Because she is me. A reflection of what I hoped I'd be. My second chance at fulfilling destiny. So, even if it is just me, pushing her, motivating her, loving her, sharing dreams with her, than there's no other place I can say I'd rather be!

- Matisha Williams

Awkward

Nerd

Trying too hard

Different

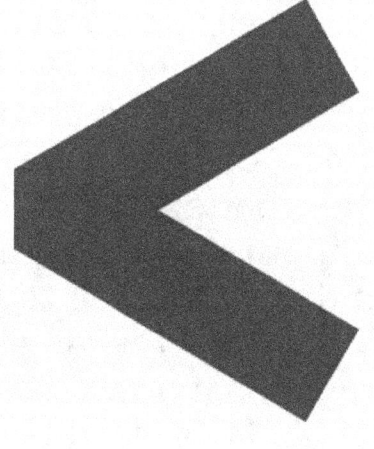

Strange

Weird

Acting White

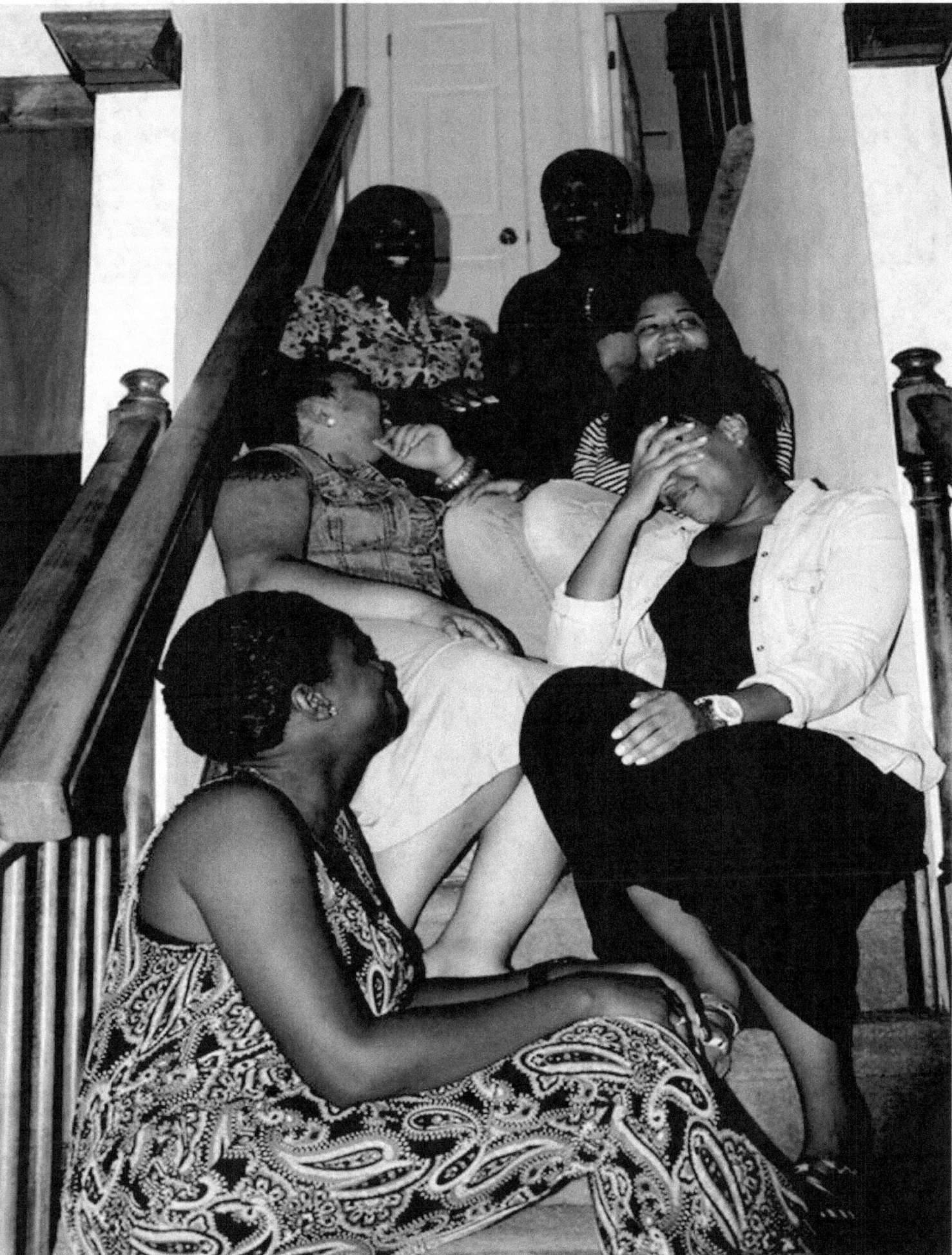

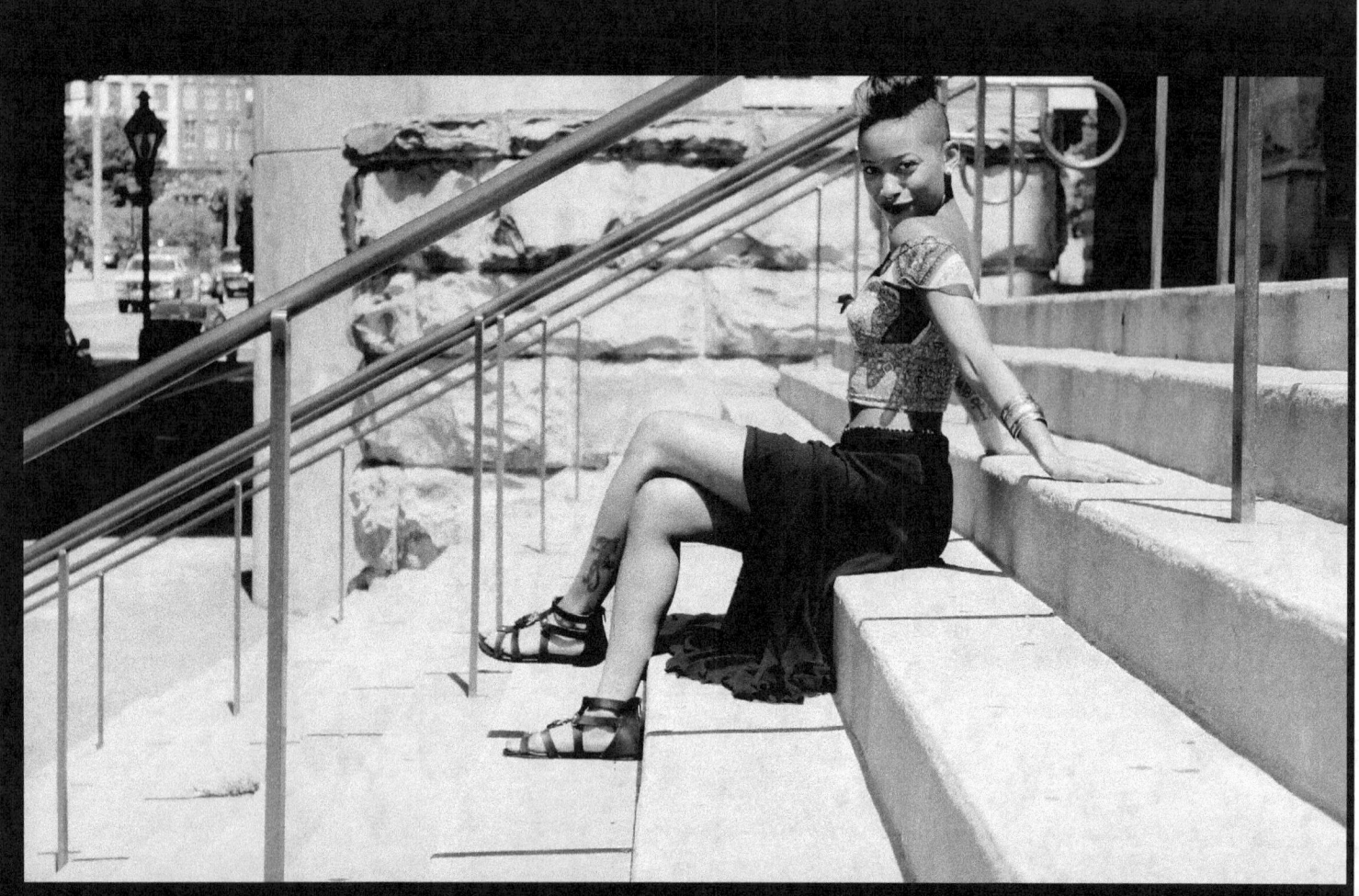

Being labeled has always been something that I've run away from. To me, labels confine you and with them, you are expected to be a certain type of person. But if you're in tune with reality, you know that we are complex creatures who change like the colors of leaves. We transform like a catapillar into a butterfly. I can't be defined by labels because everytime I have tried to call myself one thing, I grow and become something else. I once thought I was a Christian, the next year Muslim. After meeting a Jehovah witness I thought I was that too but I'm none of the above.

oTme, I am everything & I am love.   Those labels remind me that I don't have to be attached to any particular group, idea, or political party but I am free to be an individual who can get along with anyone and who is making effort to understand and respect all differences. Honestly, if people had to label me, some would say good things and some would say bad. I've been a saint and a sinner; a sweetheart and a bitch. Some call me queen and I'm sure to others I'm a peasant. Positive or negative, others' labels were never something I took to the head or heart. With labels come expectation and I prefer the beauty of the unexpected.

- B. Ross

I enjoy the shades of me
My confidence is full of pride
This ladder I've chosen to rise onto
That ceiling......well
It goes as far and as deep as I allow it to
And because I'm free in here
I'm free out here
with no fear of rejection or anti-acceptance
I am in love with me
No need to rush through this thing
because up here it's just me
And I'm taking my time for me
Too long I've lived in this box
Something always blocking me from me
Relationships. Family. A skewed view of me.
Afraid to touch my own body because I was ashamed you
see
Ashamed of me
Too many tones.
Too many dark spots.
Too many no's
Why didn't you see me?
Why not?
I finally realized my acceptance comes not from you.
But me.
An ever-evolving creature
That's me
A woman comfortable with the uncomfortable
That's me
A proper envelope pusher
That's me
Not your definition of me
That's weak
The smile on my face is genuine
I touch it as I look in the mirror and fall in love all over
again.
Not with the idea of me.
The notion of me.
The authentic, unapologetic me

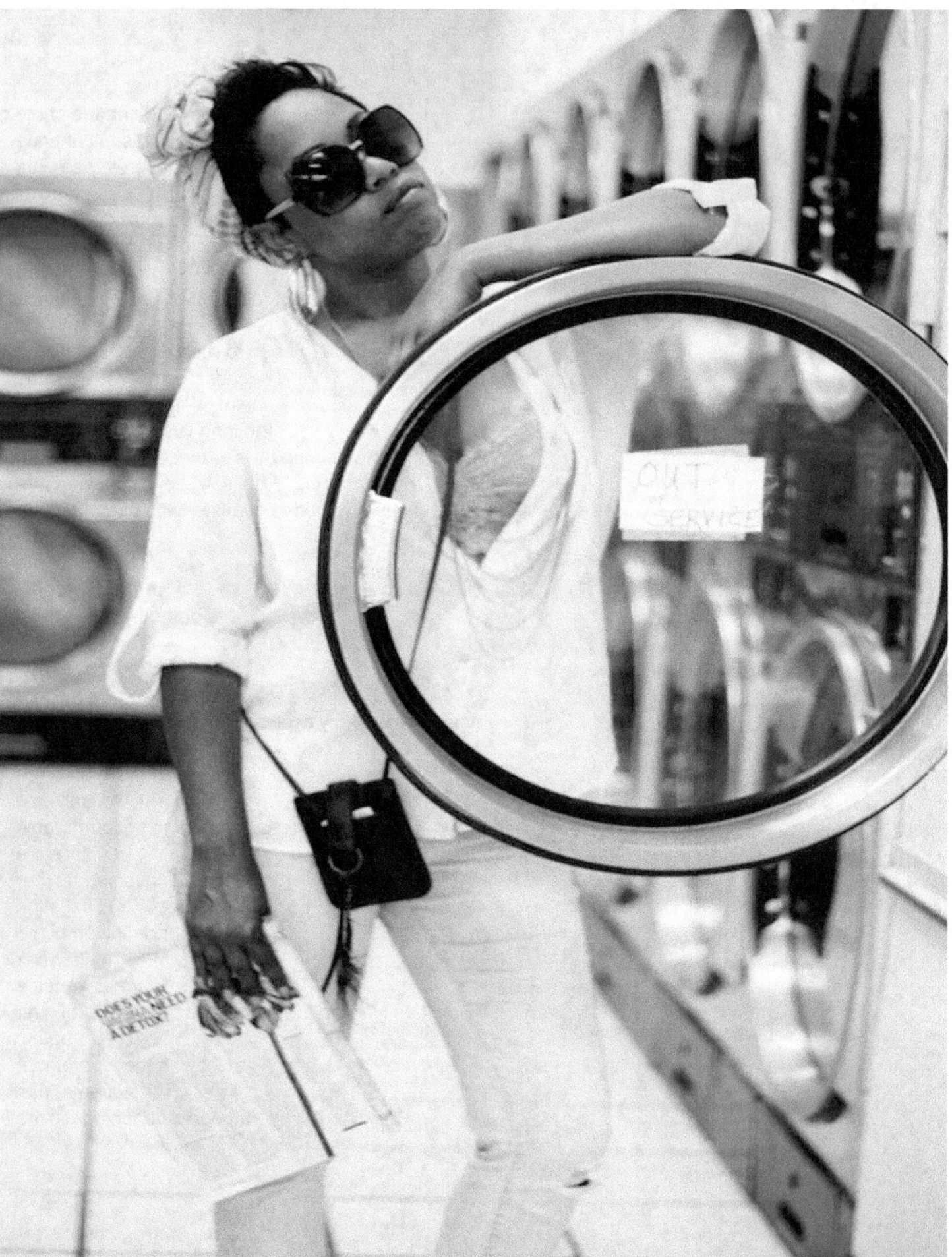

In The Wash

If I were doing my laundry
I'd wash my dirty relationships
Throw in my bad decisions and
Pour on the Ivory Soap
Scrub up my soul.
I'd wash away the knowledge of infidelity
and clean the stain of broken hearts
Rub the grease off the betrayal
Wipe up all the gossip.
Rub a dub dub misinterpretations
Flush the big empty space left behind
Rinse down my tear filled eyes
Drain the low self-esteem and make it me again.
Put some color back into my eyes
Bleach the knowledge of being one amongst many
Dump the whole mess of the past into the wringer
Squeeze out the lies
Put my heart in the dryer
and let it sit 20 minutes
Til it came out clean.

- Dominique Henry

(A play on Allen Ginsberg's, "Homework" from Collected Poems, 1947-1980.)

Tarnished crown

The pain of love and loss
Is what you get when you know you've lost
The moment when you realize you're the fool
And he'll continue to do what he do
The only real concern for him
Is how long you'll continue to give in
How long, this lesson you'll learn
Why is it for him you yearn
Are you his priority, is he really yours
Is he around to ease the boredom
The truth you know
You're feeling lonely and alone
The Queen with the tarnished crown
The one who could never be brought down
Now knows she's fallible, gullible and a whole lot of trouble
On the real, for real, throw in a double
On second thought, no, not this chick
I'm a run this shit kind of bitch
If he, him, them don't want to play
It's okay, it's a new day
I got me, from my head to my feet
I won't need you before you'll need me
I've carried the weight of the world on my shoulders
Wonder what it's like to carry boulders
Its this journey called life
Got no choice but to live it
The last thing I need to do is give in
If I don't fit your mold then break it
I'm that chic who'll stick by you and help you make it
But there's only some much bullshit I can take and
If that's not good enough for you then fake it, for yourself
It's time to please me above everyone else
It's time for me to do my thing and bring the house down,
I'm no longer the queen with the tarnished crown

- Queen Johnson

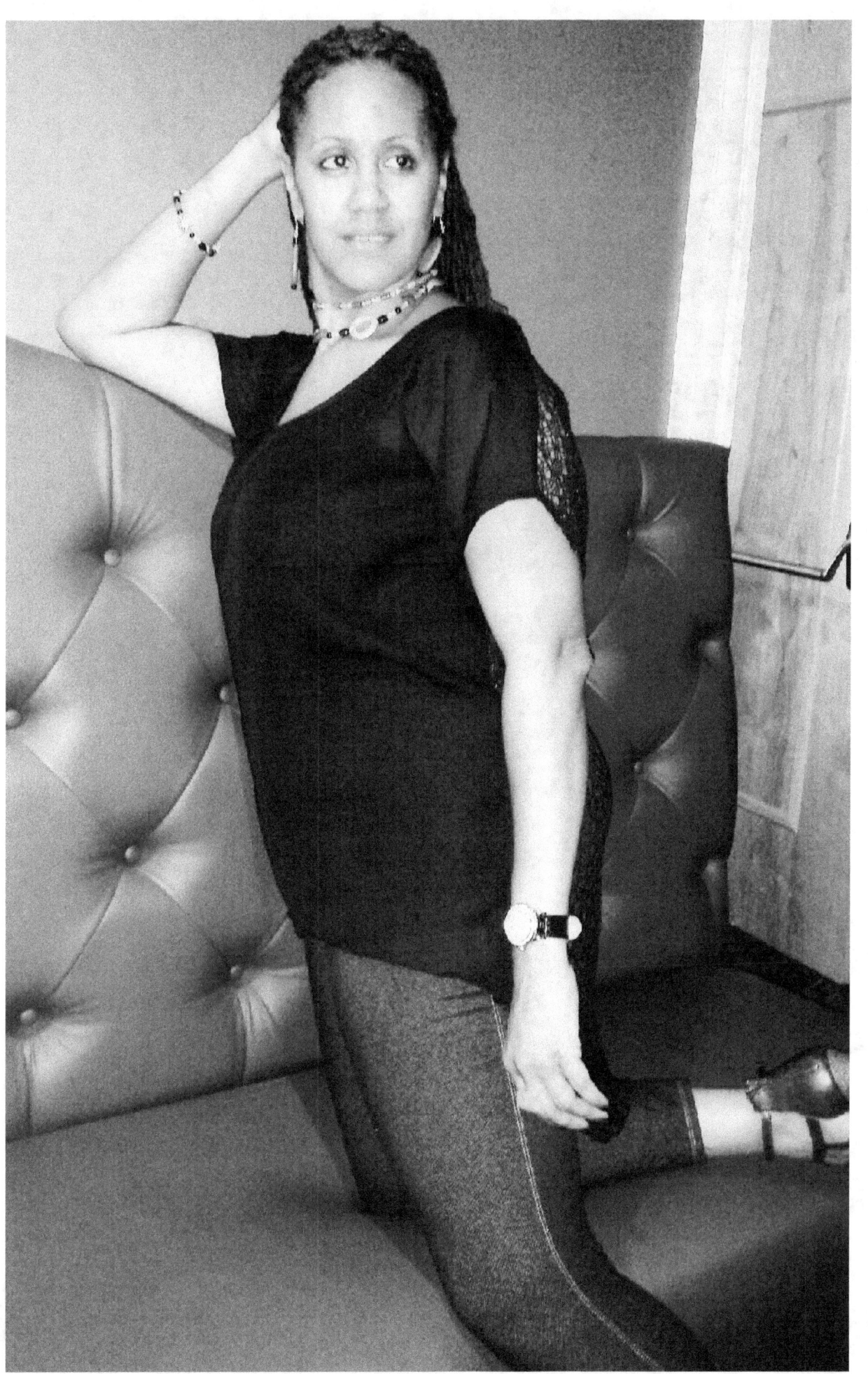

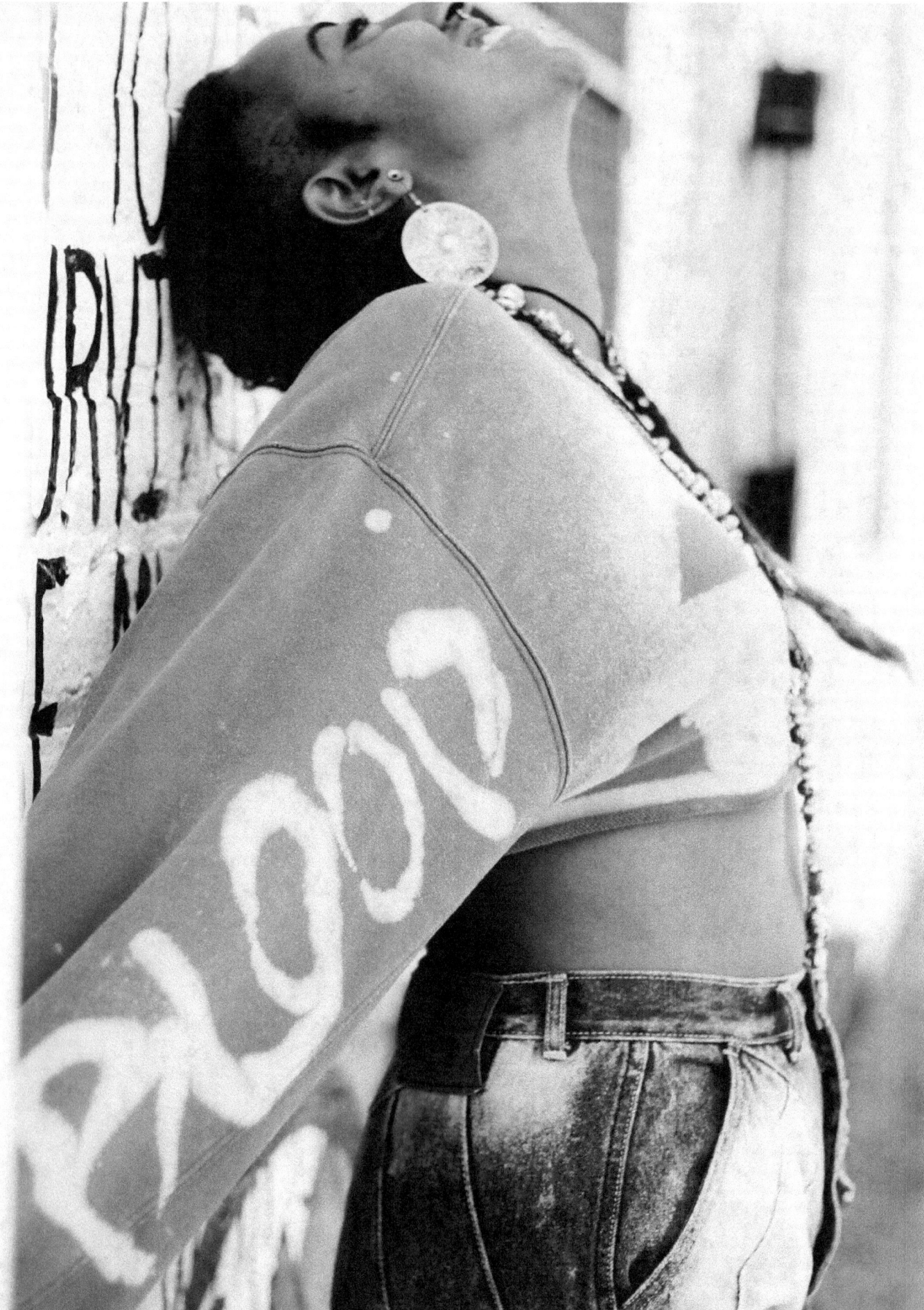

Maruim Eltahir

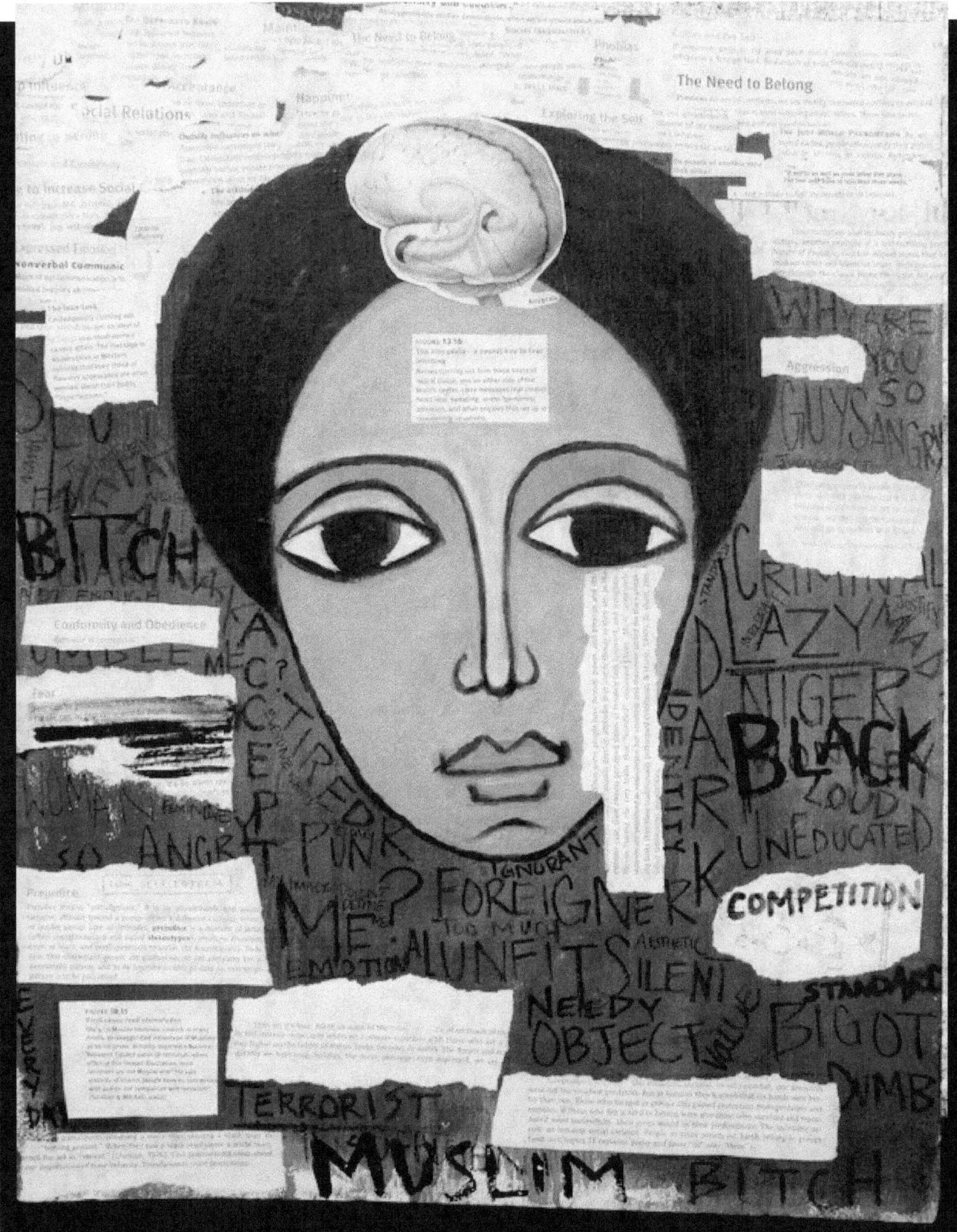

Mixed Media piece by
Maruim Eltahir
titled
"Lazy Terrorist Bitch",
representing her
personal labels as a
black Muslim woman.

Lighting Cigarettes

Unless you know her
Stayed aboard and didn't jump ship
When she became unfamiliar
When it became uncomfortable to bear
The topic of conversations that did nothing to help
When she stopped being someone you understood
When her faculties left
Her love for self diminished
When she no longer was who you thought she should be
The dreams faded
Bitterness grew
And all that mattered was the drink on the table
Don't comment about her to me

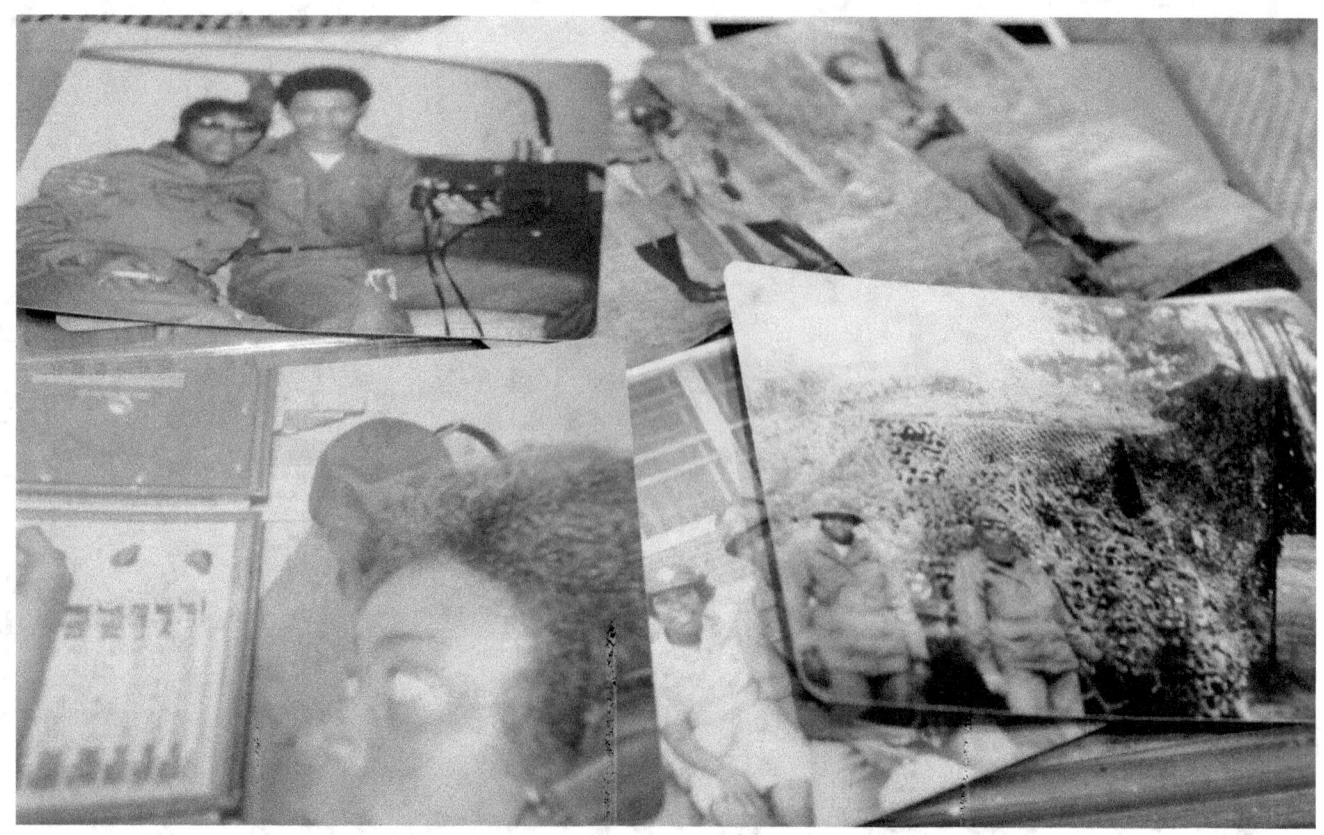

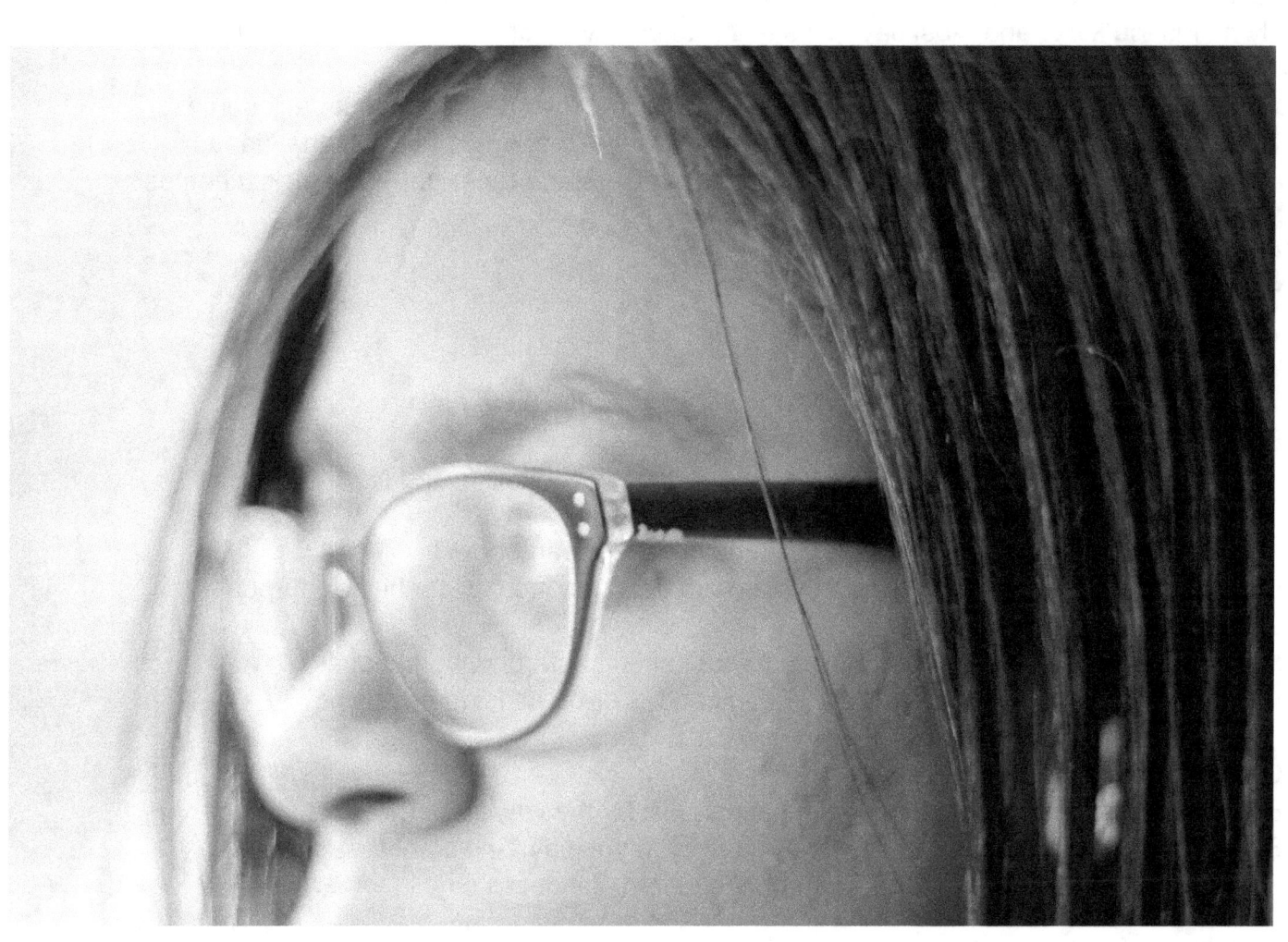

She's Not That Cute Anyway

My mother use to pinch my nose when I was a child
Said it was too wide
My hair is too kinky and most days I'd say it's actually very dry
I have full lips and when I'm nervous I bite the bottom one
My hips are full and after staring into the mirror too long I've decided to cut back some
The video vixens and the latest bad _itches don't have to struggle to get in their jeans
I don't make enough money to spend on waist cinchers and other get-fine-quick schemes
Most days I have four eyes
And even then I still squint to see…
Shades are always trending
When being "light" was in I didn't fit in
When being "dark" was in I didn't fit in
Too ashamed for two pieces because of the stretch marks on my skin
Pretty average girl but there's always been a fire within
Face spotted with blemishes that I never chose to hide with MAC and Nars
I've always looked down when asked about my scars
My polish is usually chipped and my teeth have never been perfect
But even though I'm an average girl I've always been in touch with a higher purpose
Confidence is intimidating
I know a little about a lot so I don't have to get naked to start conversations
A woman that always has a book in her bag can never be considered "basic"
I don't have to comb my naps
Or have perfectly arched brows
Because people can see the spirit of a woman just by the way she smiles
So thank you very much for all the times I've heard you say "she's not that cute anyway"
Being an absolutely phenomenal woman beats cute any damn day

- Teshawn Butler

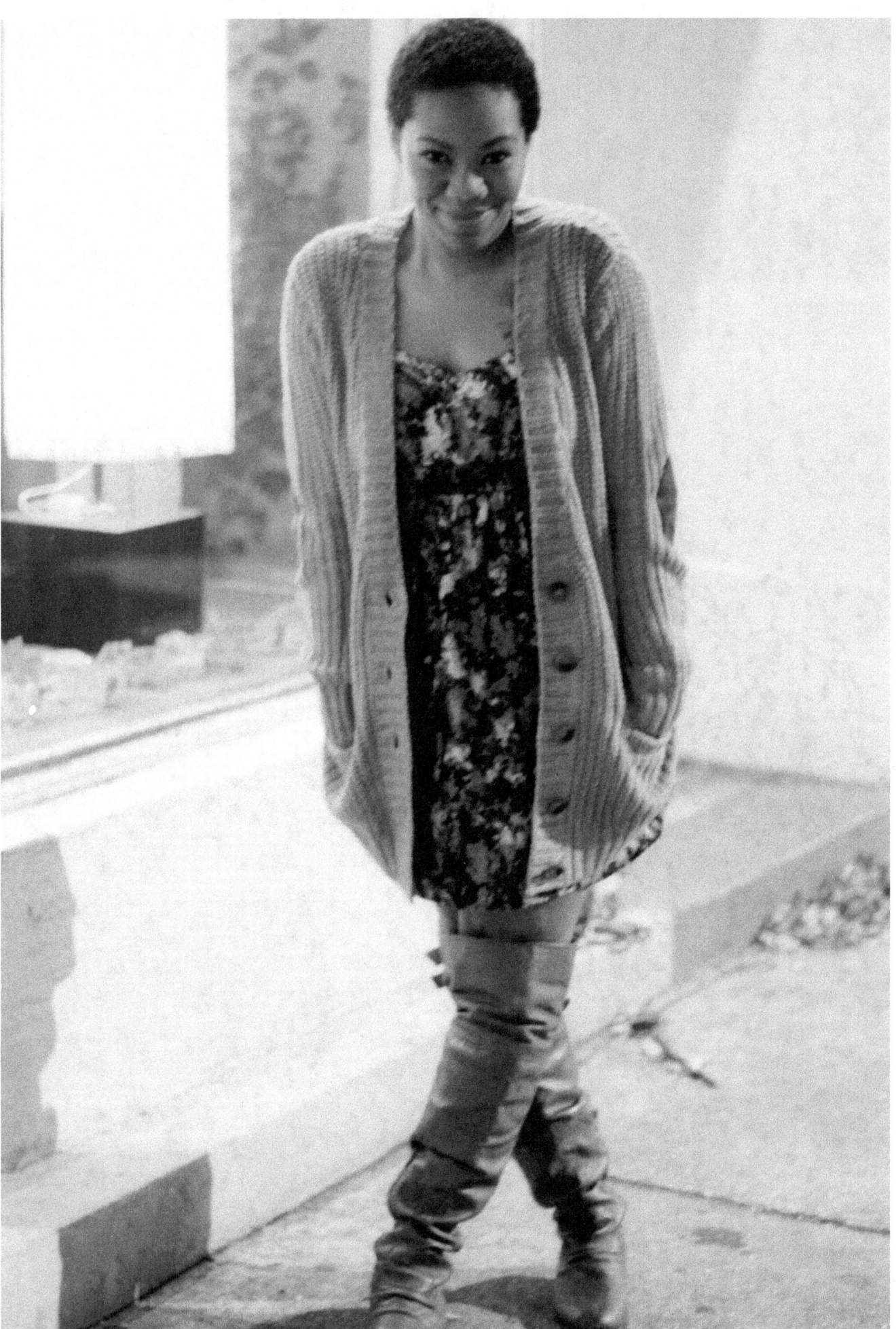

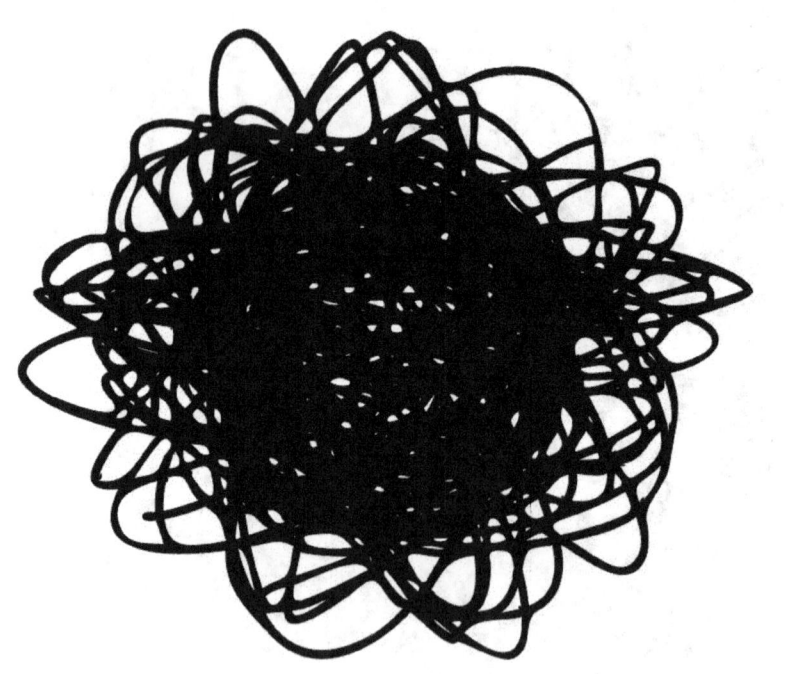

"You tell me
how to stop thinking.
We're writers!
All we do is think!"

one day i want to be barefoot with flowers in my hair and the next i want to twerk and wear fake nails. i am a complex multi dimensional being, no labels can and should be put on me! or you!! We all have so many different aspects of ourselves, no need to put it all in a category. Lets live label free. < 3
~~~~

5 notes

Music defines me. I've been singing since I was 4 years old, funny part is my parents had no clue. I wasn't classically trained, or brought up in intricate programs to develop my craft, I wasn't sent to a special school. I merely had a kindergarten teacher who believed in me. So when she said sing, I opened my mouth because the fear and respect she instilled in me wasn't like anything that children learn today. I stepped forward and sung, and my parents mouths dropped in awe.

Let's fast forward: 19 years, multiple choirs, piano lessons, volleyball teams, scholastic awards, scholarships, a bad record deal and a failed quartet later. Twenty three years old and I've created a small business called La Dainta Vintage. I'm being labeled a stylist, a vintage connoisseur, a fashion guru. There are 4,446 people that follow me on instagram but don't even know me. They see clothes and jewelry and photographs of beautiful women. They've labeled me a fashionista and diva in this community and they think this must be the life. She has a successful business and she's involved in so much and everyone knows her, but in reality I'm trapped. I'm trapped in the labels I've been given. All I really want to do is sing. I was born to, created to, gifted to just sing. The more I participate in labeling myself as a stylist and small business owner, the more I suffer as an artist.

Music is what makes me weird and awkward.
Music is what let's me know I'm alive.
Music is my outlet.
Music is the label I want.
Music is what defines me.

- Andrea Nicole

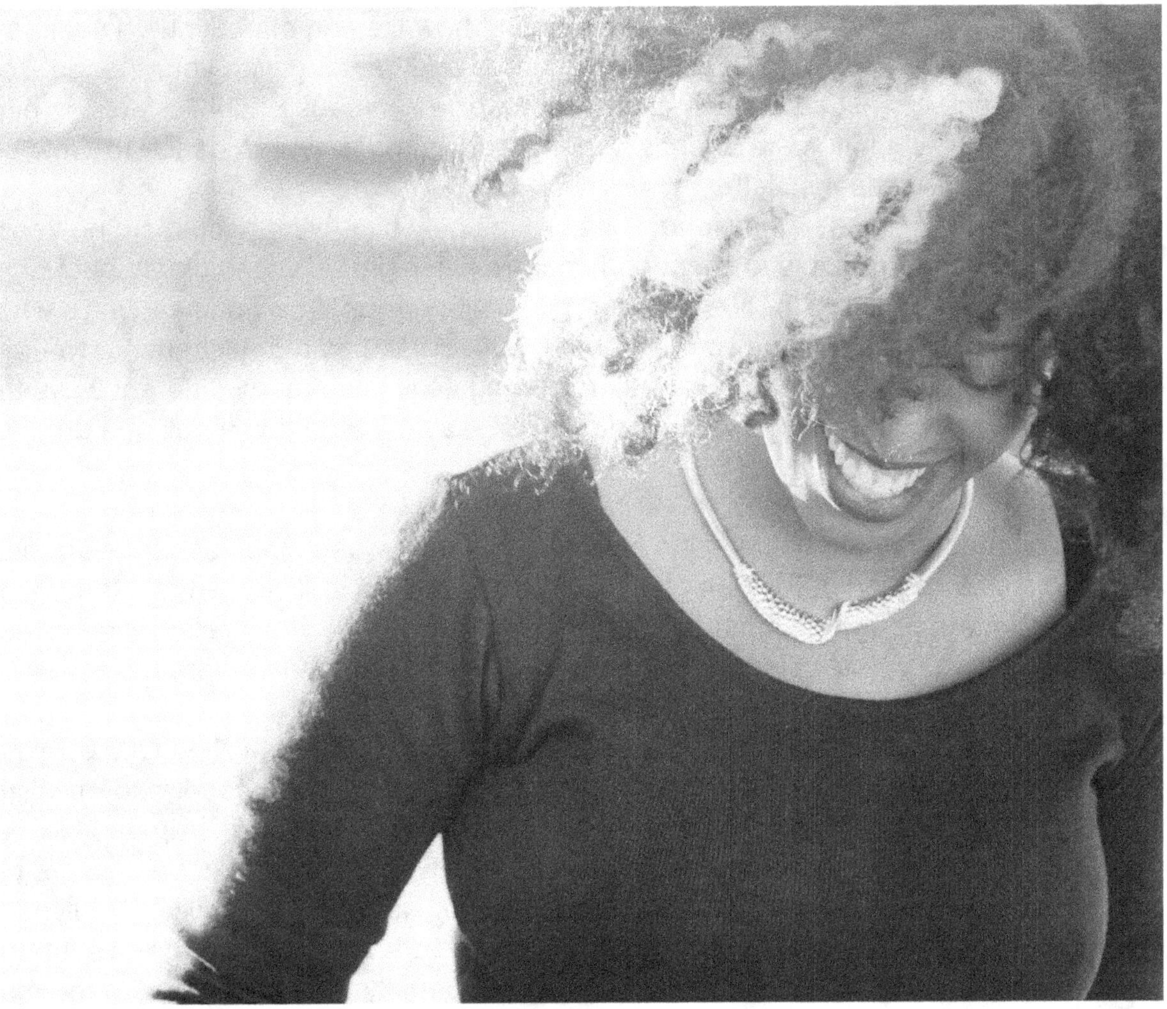

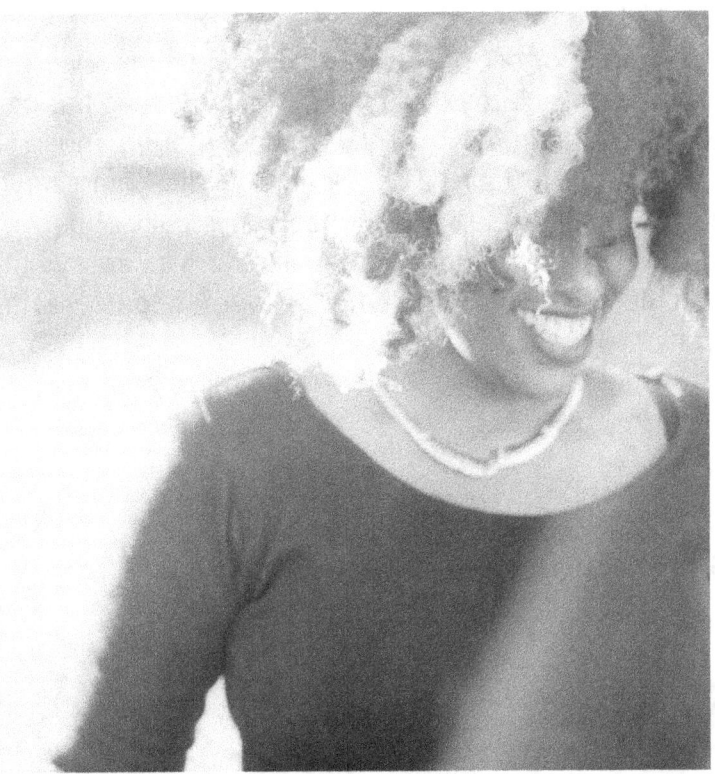

When you are a kid, you never have any idea of how life can affect you. In your youth, life is all about riding bikes, skipping rocks, climbing trees and hanging with your friends. You just don't know how one event that happens to someone else can cause ripple effects so big, so massive, that it changes your life permanently. When I was young, I had no desire to grow up fast. I didn't want to become responsible for

anyone else, much less a household. Hell, I was only nine! What could a nine year-old do? Yeah, my mother taught me how to cook (and cook well, I might add) and clean, but I didn't know how to do much else outside of roller skating and jumping rope. In a nutshell, that's what happened to me. Life reared its ugly head so much that I had to make so many changes. Not only that, it would become a cycle that would keep repeating itself in so many different ways that it's a wonder that I didn't lose my mind. Or did I? I will say this: Faith is a hell of a drug! One that I will never give up!

"I was booooorn by the river"...well, not really. Ok, no I wasn't, but it sounded good! I was actually born in a little section of Eastern Henrico County, Virginia, called Central Gardens in 1975. I was the third of four daughters born to my parents, Stephen and Rita Bailey. When I was four, my family moved to Western Henrico County, where my sisters and I were raised until we were grown. My mother was a

social worker for the Juvenile Courts and my father worked at the Post Office. We had a pretty good life. My family lived in a very nice, up-and-coming neighborhood, and my sisters and I attended some really good schools. We had a very good life growing up and we didn't want for anything. Now, don't get me wrong, I loved my family, but we were not as picture perfect as my father would have liked people to believe. My father was very controlling. He lived by the principle that the man was the head of the household and was in charge of everything. He was the king of his castle and we were his subjects. Normally, the theory/idea of the man being the head would not be an issue for me. My problem was how it was perpetuated. My father ran his home more like a dictatorship than a monarchy.

What he said was law. It didn't matter how wrong or out of line he was, it was his way. Period. No ifs, ands, or buts. I loved my daddy because he was...my daddy. A girl's first love is her daddy and he could do no wrong. My daddy was the man in my eyes. Over time, though, those feelings changed and our relationship deteriorated...fast. Basically, what went on in the home stayed in the home, and he better not hear about it from anyone else. He wasn't physically abusive, but the mental and emotional treatment was horrible. My father seemed like he was always mad or upset all the time. I rarely saw him smile unless he was doing what he wanted to do. Matter of fact, I never really saw my father show any

other kind of emotion other than anger. I would later find out that he was more sad and disenchanted

about events that happened in his life.

Although I wasn't told a lot, what I did find out made a little bit of sense. I'll touch more on that later.

My mother, on the other hand, she was something else. I loved that woman to pieces! Like Keith Murray said, to me, she was "the most beautifullest thing in this world"! Mommies always made everything all right, and my momma was no different. This woman would work 8-5 Monday through Friday, come home and put together a smorgasbord of a meal, and still have energy to help with homework, give us baths, make desserts, and read us a bedtime story. She would show up for plays, kiss our boo-boos, take us to Girl Scouts and all. Rita Grace was an angel on Earth, however, she did not shy away from discipline. Whatever she could get her hands on, she immediately became a samurai warrior, Hank Aaron or Nolan Ryan, if you will. She did not hesitate to make you go get your own switch (and it better be right when you gave it to her) when you done plucked her nerves enough or you just didn't do what was asked of you. My mother taught me the art of the roundhouse from the front seat. Oh, that woman was sick with it, let me tell you! But my momma was so big on family. She made it a point to visit my aunts that lived in DC almost every weekend. Her father, my grandaddy, lived less than 5 minutes from us and he was pretty darned awesome, too. Anytime any one of the kids in our family had a birthday, all of my mother's family showed up. The bond between my mother and her siblings (all six of them) is the kind of bond I hope my sisters and I, as well as our children, will have and more.

As I mentioned before, I have three sisters: Jessica, Caroline, and Vanessa.
Jessica, the eldest, was the "brains" and the "responsible" one. She was always in charge when my parents were working or out and about. She had to make sure that the rest of us, especially the younger two, did our chores, homework, and ate dinner. Caroline, was the "socialite" and the "rebel without a pause", for lack of a better
description. That girl was always into something. Always. From sneaking out to sneaking people in, she always had something going on. I will admit, she could organize some of the best basement parties I ever knew of, as long as I didn't snitch to my daddy (he worked the night shift so she really had nothing to worry about). I will also admit that it was because of her that I didn't get to enjoy some privileges or rites of passage. I mean, just because she "stole" my daddy's van to go to a college homecoming game, I should not have been banned from getting my driver's license! Okay, it's safe to say I haven't really gotten over that incident. But c'mon, really though? I ain't even do nothing! Lastly, there was Vanessa. She was the "baby" and pretty much had everything done for her. By me, of course. Vanessa had a bit of a learning disorder, so she was catered to a lot. I say a little bit because she knows full well what she does and is doing, but the consequence really don't sink in. She has a limited capacity to process much of the information that is given to her at any time. But she can definitely get by doing what she knows how to do.
So where do I fit in? I dunno, really. I won't call myself the "black sheep" because of the negative undertones, and I am not a bad person. Well, not that bad anymore. I guess I would say I am the "forgotten" or "old reliable". I didn't really have a title back then growing up. I just know that everyone kept telling me that, no matter what happened, they knew I would be alright. I guess I am the "alright" one? I know I would always make sure that everyone else was alright. There were so many times in my life that I wished people didn't know that I would be alright. I wished they would actually ask me if I was instead of assuming. It felt like I was there, but wasn't, rather, no one could see me or would pay me any mind because they were so busy tending to my sisters. Such is the life of the second middle child.

It was the end of March in 1984 and it was my ninth birthday. I was feeling good. We were at McDonald's and we were having a party. My birthday party. For those of you who don't understand, you had to have it going on back then to have a party at McDonald's! But I was the ish because I had Ronald McDonald AND Grimace there! What?!? You couldn't tell me nothing! All my aunts and uncles were there, my sisters my daddy. I was almost the perfect day. I said almost because she wasn't there. I kept looking around to see if she was going to walk in at any minute, but she didn't. I already knew she wouldn't. Wishful thinking, I guess. I knew full well that my momma was in the hospital and she wouldn't be well enough to come outside and play. To me, it was more like punishment than being sick.

This is the same woman who never missed a birthday. She would make or buy a cake for whichever child's birthday it was and we would celebrate. That was better than the McDonald's birthday party, in all honesty. It ain't a party unless Rita Bailey was there. I tried to have fun. I mean, hey, my daddy pretty much pulled all the stops in what I now realized was his attempt at keeping my mind off of what was going on with my mother. I had recently begun noticing things. I remember I asked my mommy one day how it was possible that she could take her hair off but I couldn't? How come she was tired all the time nowadays and couldn't come to school as much anymore? That was also around the time that I began sleepwalking and wound up in my parent's bed in the middle of the night and my daddy having to put me back in my own bed (I woke up a couple of times during the transition). I remember that I would get mad at him in my dreams for taking me away from my mommy. Maybe I knew something was about to happen, but didn't know, ya know?

Fast forward three months and it was now June. My daddy took us up to St. Luke's Hospital, on the fifth floor. We sat in the waiting area. Well, my daddy and older sisters sat, while Vanessa and I were just busy. I guess we were just too excited for what was about to happen. I remember it seemed like it had been an eternity since the last time. I just couldn't wait. The anticipation was killing me. I had so much I wanted to share...so much to say! In the midst of all these thoughts going through my mind, I heard the door open. I spun around and there she was! Rita in-all-her Grace Bailey! My momma! I wanted to run and jump into her arms, but I was warned that I needed to take it easy and be gentle. She hasn't gotten her strength back yet. No one had yet to tell me exactly what was wrong with her. I guess at that age, we still needed to be spoon-fed the truth. Anyway, I didn't care. My momma was right here in front of me and I can touch her and talk to her! She had forgotten to put her hair back on and she looked feeble and pale, but she was still beautiful to me! I don't think I took a breath while I was telling her all the excitement that she had been missing, including that awesome party at McDonald's that she missed. I remember I sat in the chair next to her the whole time. I grabbed her arm and never let go the whole time. I was "alright" just sitting there. I didn't really hear what anyone else was talking about...I tuned them out. We must have been there for what felt like hours because the next thing I remember is my momma kissing me on the forehead and telling me she loves me. It was time to go and I was waiting on her to get her stuff and come on. Instead, she had to stay. I was mad. Shoot, I was HOT! I asked her when she would be going home because I was tired of her being gone all the time. She said soon. Little did I

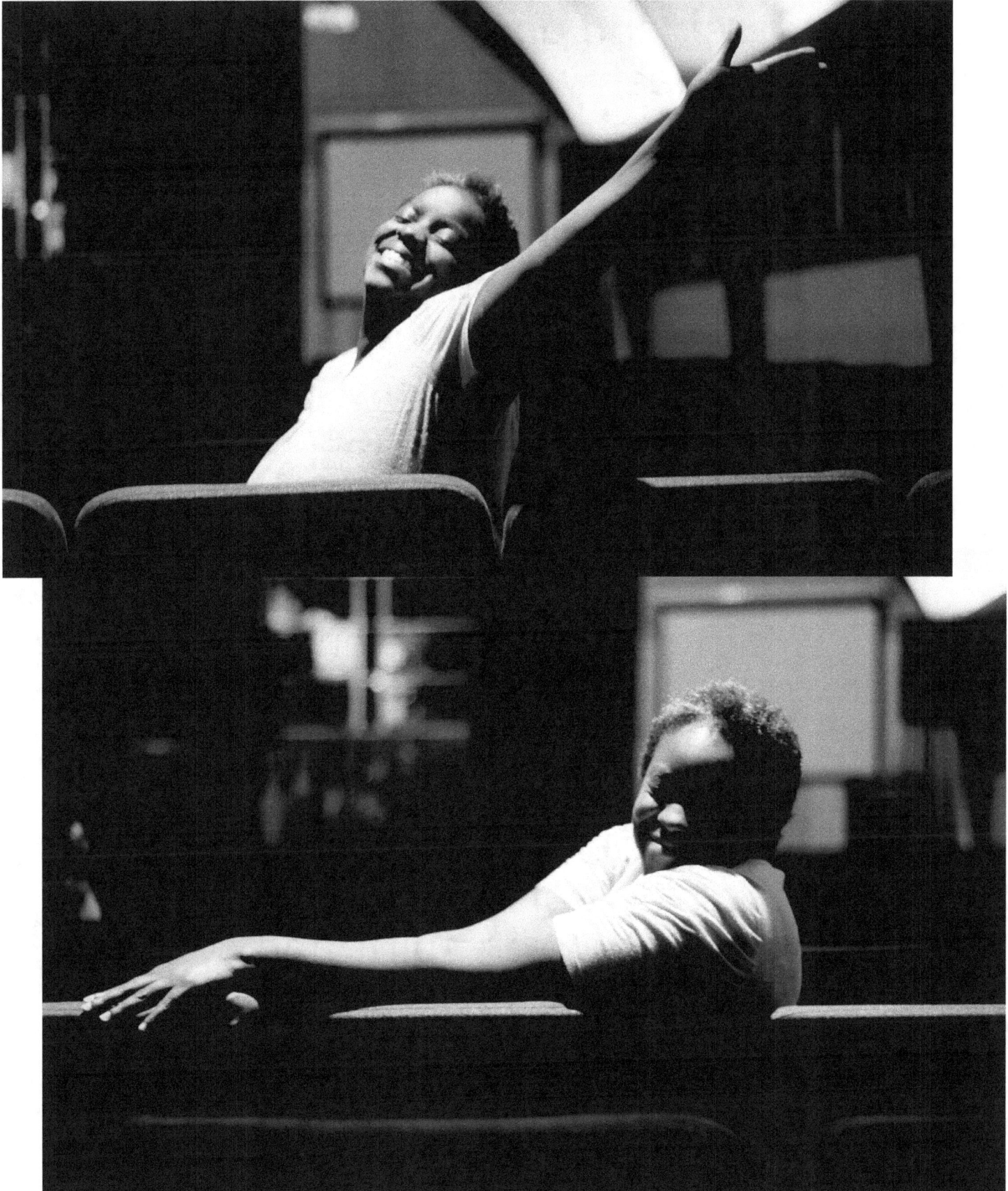

All I think about is
sex and empowerment
Queen wanting to be
in submission
Crossing the lines of
flesh and moans
Skin and sin
The case to own
the light between my thighs
Can sexy be hidden
behind my speeches?
Heels covering the
cries to be heard
Here doesn't belong
to a church
Up for discussion
and passed as a basket
It belongs to God
I dare say it also belongs to me
Division between spirit and soul
I lie next to me every night
And feel flesh
no one else is touching
And think why not

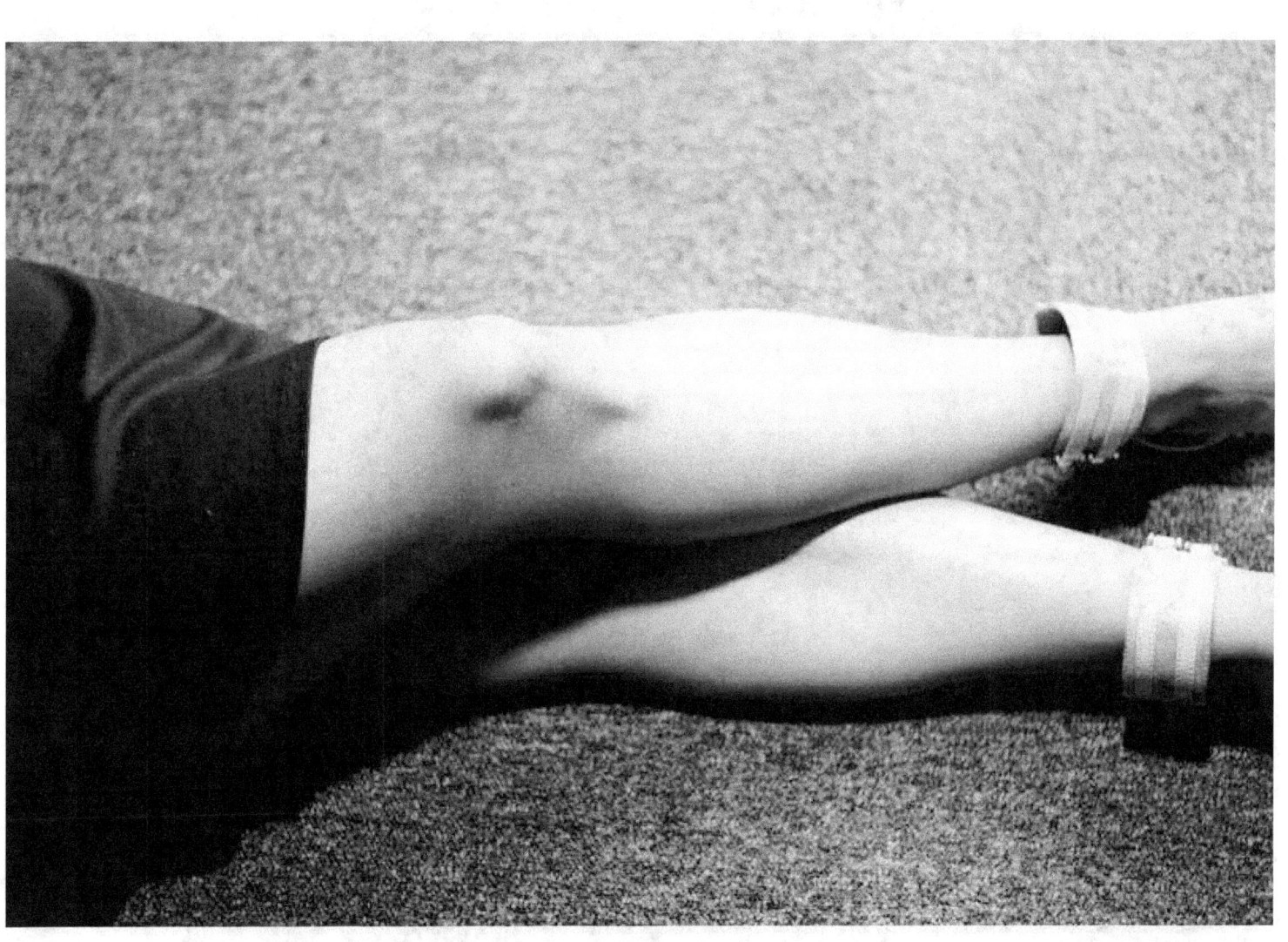

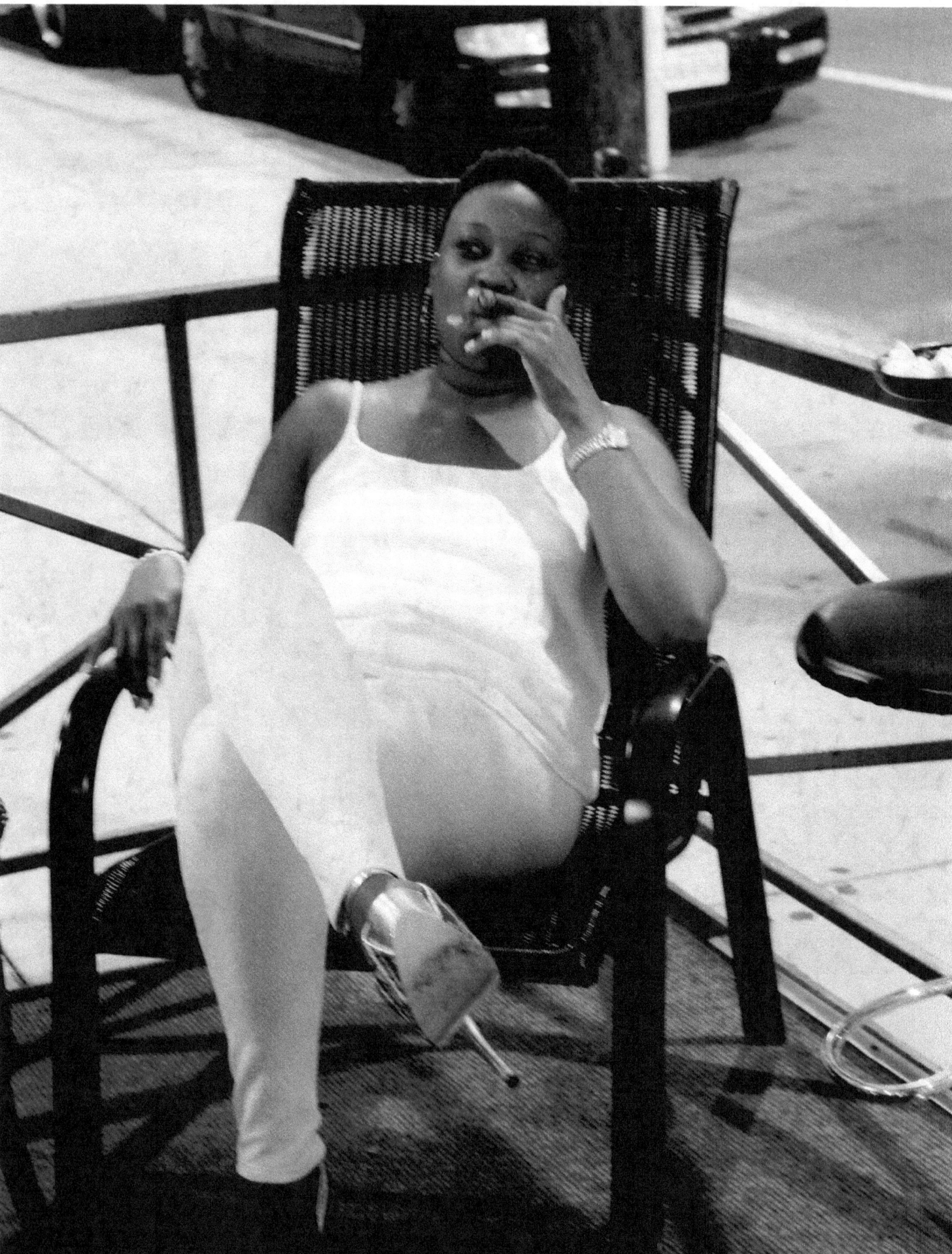

My cigar smokin and bible totin self
My southern drawl havin, shuckin and jivin self
Music lovin, kid totin self
Inconsistent, ever present self
Bible quotin, ever jokin self
Cookie burnin, ever lovin self
Broken pieces, bein mended self
Front porch sittin, stiff drink sippin self
Lash doin, church croonin self
God fearin, child rearin self
Ever dreamin, faith believen, success seekin, God pleasing self
Not bitter, gettin encouragement, givin self

- Nudasha Gratic-Fludd

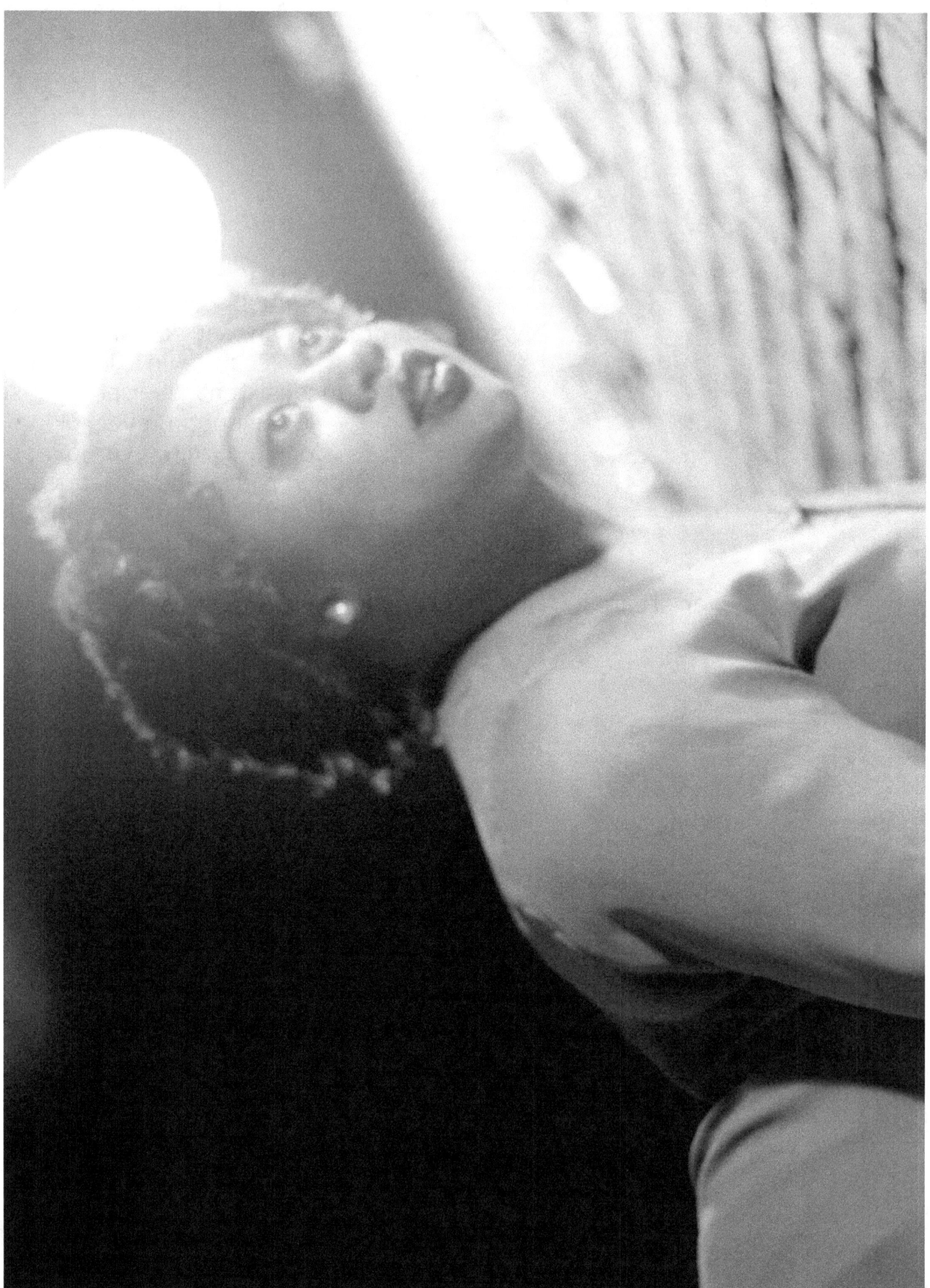

I'm too forgiving. I've been hurt a lot in the past. And I'm always there at the end of the day as if it never happened. But you'll never know by looking at me. I smile and keep it moving. I go so hard for myself and have never been the person to receive handouts and I give a lot as well. It's difficult for me to say no to anyone in fear of making someone upset or angry. I do a lot of talking and praying. My grandmother and I share a lot. We talk and try to give a good reason as to why what has happened in my life has happened, but at the end of the search, I try to block out the negative and focus on my wellbeing. Since then, I've been able to do some major things! I've taken classes, about to start school again, a new job and career path. Just by a lot of self-love and not looking to anyone for approval.

- Christina White

You're putting more attention on your exterior
than your interior
I see you shaking your derriere
but how you expect to draw a King
when that ain't rare
Don't you know how to draw a king
with garbs of self respect to get that ring?
How you expect to draw a king when you're a slave girl
and started off a queen?
A slave girl
A slave to today's perception of beauty
You replaced your crown with a highlighted synthetic 25 inch
definition of what society thinks beauty is
A slave to a mask
You replaced your flawless skin
with chemicals for a lighter solution
Those same chemicals are what has caused
a self racist pollution
You're replacing your naturally rose colored lips
with black soot
Simultaneously trying to strap someone else's likes
to your foot
I see you dropping it like it's hot
for Champagne and Money
But how you expect to draw a King
when he's looking for the scent
of milk and honey

- Janay Hargrove

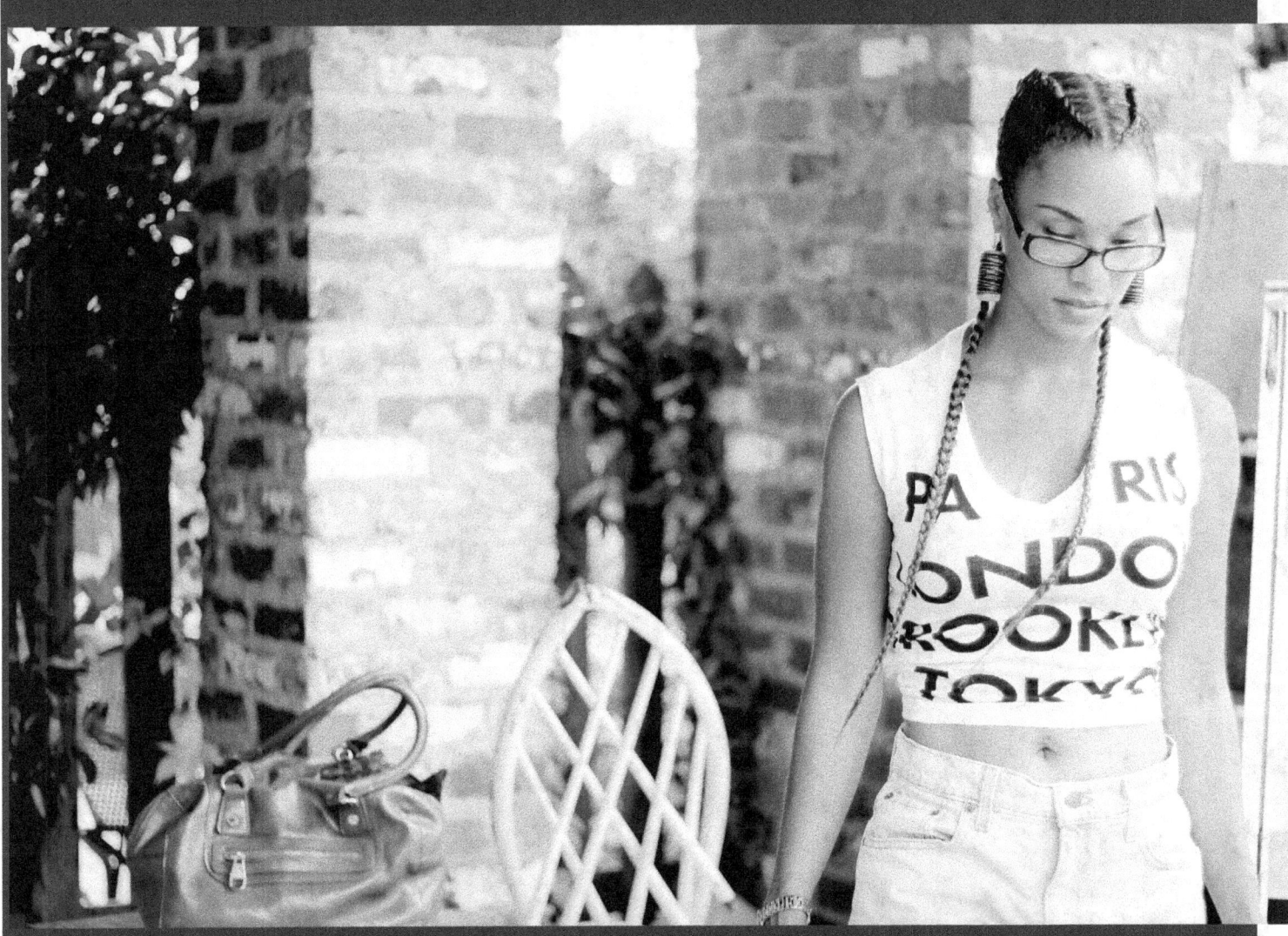

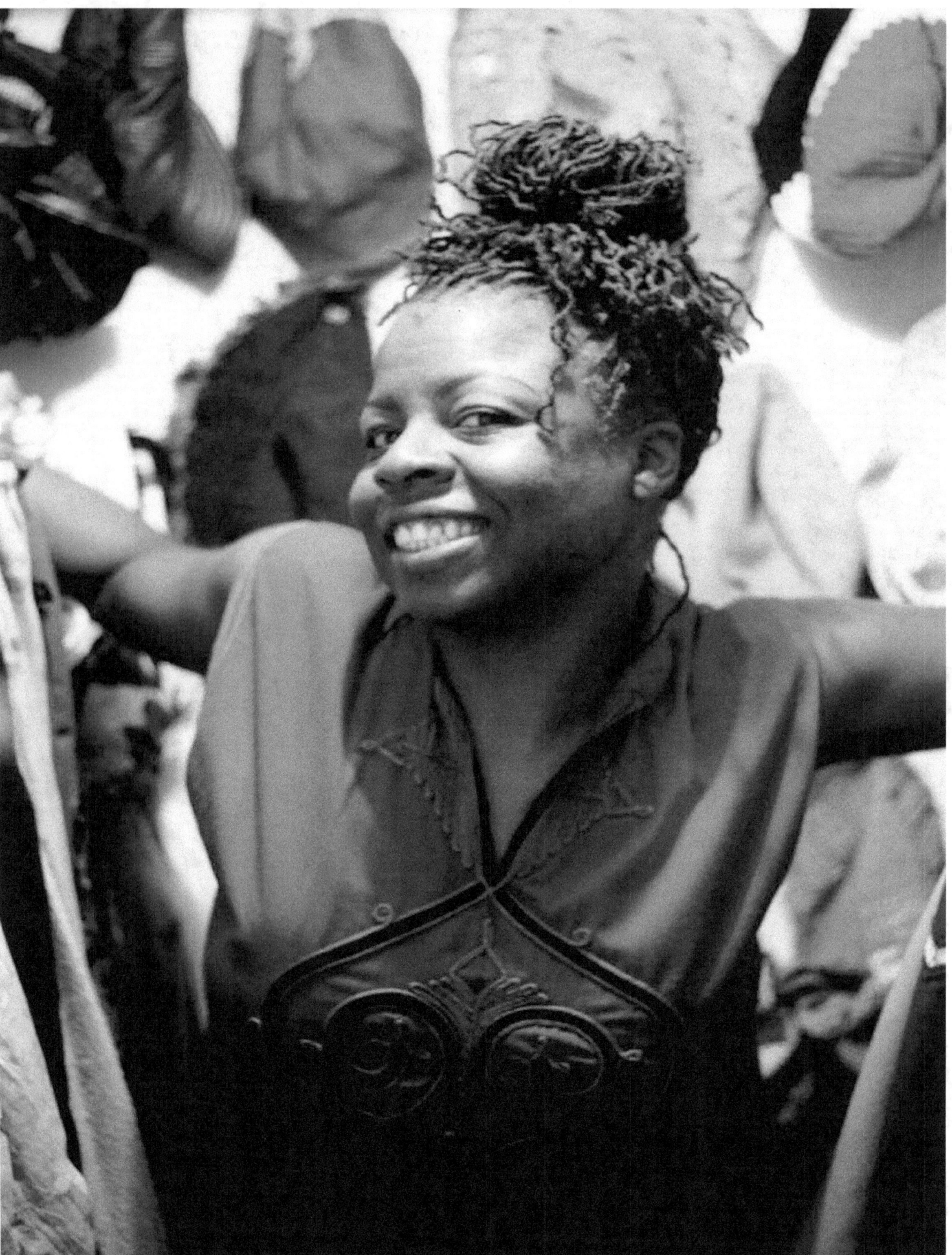

had an awakening recently.

Saying "how I got over" is a little too passive for me. That implies that somebody might have been pulling me or I'd been trudging up and then slid back down the mountain and just happened to somehow accidently slip over the summit. I'm not passive. I fought through that mountain. I didn't climb the mountain, I fought through it. I fought kicking and fighting and screaming and crying. Tae Kwon Do and nun chucks. I knocked some mountains out of the way. I adopted a warrior stance the day I went up against the mountain of fists bigger than mine flying towards me and declared that I will never be beat again. Leveling mountains became part of my permanent physiological make-up. I am a fighter.

Now here I am, years later, and I've realized something; I don't know how to not fight. No, I don't go around actively seeking a battle but I have learned that without confrontation, there can be no peace and because I want that peace, I aggressively confront confusion, time and time again. I live that philosophy and yet am such a peace-loving person. How does that work? Lol. Well, I stay continually poised for scenarios in which I'd need to do battle for the sake of that peace, always primed, always alert, and yet I'm good with that? Yes, I am. If you don't confront an issue, it thrives and jacks you up.

Then one day, I went to spend some time with a friend who didn't have a need to be taken care of. There were no impending battles that I needed to gear up for. His skirmishes were his own and he was more than fully capable taking care of them without my assistance. That never happens. I had nothing to confront before I (we) could take my (our) peace! I just...was.

Most of my life, I've always found myself having to take care of everybody, that I've have to be Mama Nickey, Aunt Nickey, Mentor, Counselor, Caretaker, Big Sister Nickey, but in those moments, with that friend, I didn't have a need to tend to therefore I didn't need to be any of those things. If he was comfortable, if I was comfortable, we could just play. And rest. Wait, rest? I didn't know what to do with
that. There was nothing to fight there yet, tell me how do you not fight when all you know is battle? Hey, I've been combating for the Nobel Peace Prize for 40 years so what do you mean I don't have to fight?!

During that time with him, I unzipped my chest and the armor just fell off. I floundered for the figurative blanket to cover my exposed abdomen but immediately kicked it off because I felt like I was being smothered by this foreign object and here I was, still bare, no battle armor, no weapons, just me. Suddenly, I didn't have to engage in someone's war, fighting so that they wouldn't have to fight alone, as much...or even not at all. I didn't have to fight. I could just let the sun rise and set without taking care of him or even myself. I could just be. There was a new type of peace in that. It was awesome.

Everything in life isn't excellent; sometimes you wake up mad, somebody makes you mad, bills due, stuff breaks down, kids get on your nerves, whatever. Life ain't always excellent-but I am excellent in it. I choose to be an excellent person in this life. Despite it all, I have the power of forgiveness to keep me consistently in the light so that's where I live. I didn't survive rape, physical abuse, emotional neglect, suicidal depression, homelessness, molestation for nothing! I carry absolutely NO bones about it. I'm not damaged – I'm healed. Delivered. FREE. I fought for this freedom. I fought for this peace. I beat up conflict to release this peace that I'ma keep on sharing.

And I won.
And it was worth it.

'Cause I would take nothing for my journey now.**
That ain't nothin' but a word Maya.

- Nickey "Nak" McMullen
**Credit: Maya Angelou novel title

The label I receive most is freedom - how free I am. That I tend to not care about the opinions of others and just flow through life uninhibited.
To get to even the appearance of that fact has not been easy.

Separation and divorce began my freedom. I started to see color again. My life up to that point had been black and white with massive splotches of gray. I had to teardown the castles I'd built of my marriage; the ideals and identity I'd been holding on to, and get down to my foundation - whatever that was. I discovered I love to dance. I love to take road trips to bookstores and stashed away foodie destinations. I love my chai tea with almond milk. I'm a worshipper. An introvert. An author/poet/photographer. I've survived divorce. I've survived emotional abuse. I keep going when every nerve in my body screams there's no hope. And here I am today. Healthier. Wiser.
Still making mistakes but now I note them as invaluable lessons

If this is the look of freedom, may it always have flawless sarcasm and a deep wine lip.

- Joi Donaldson

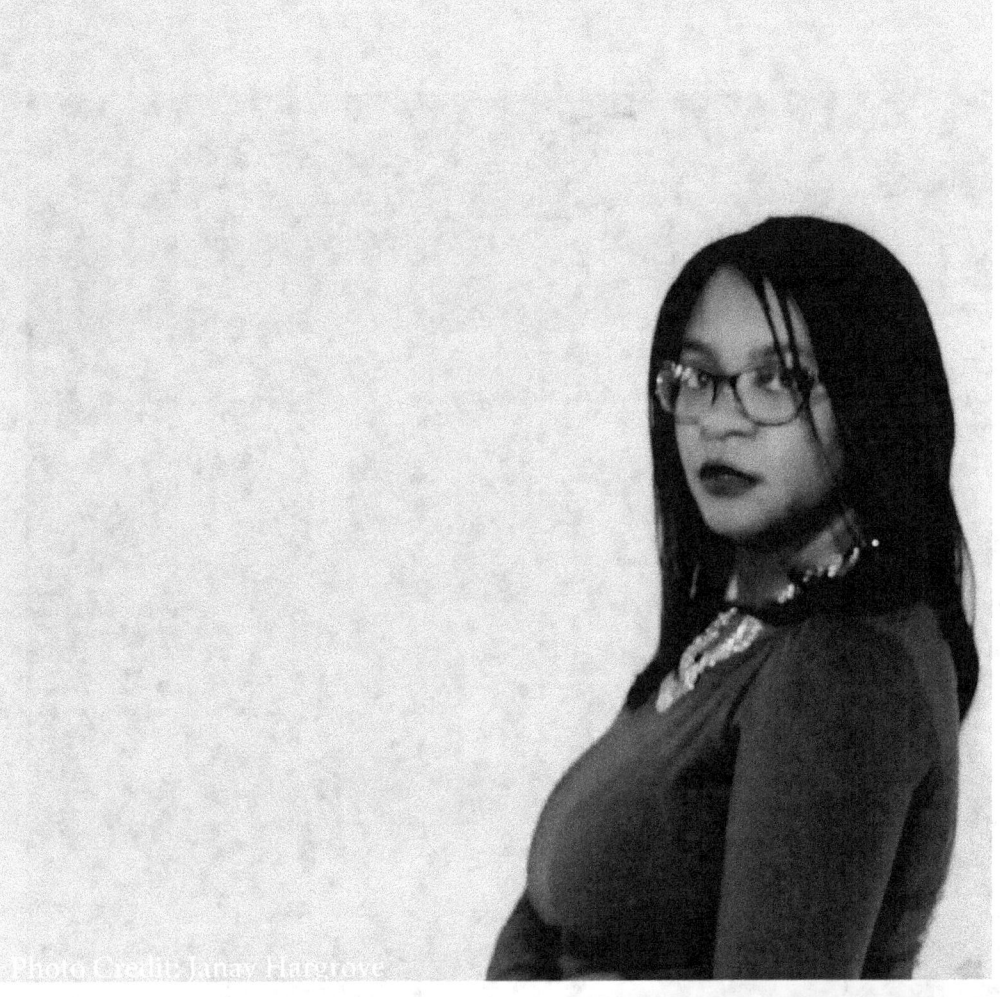

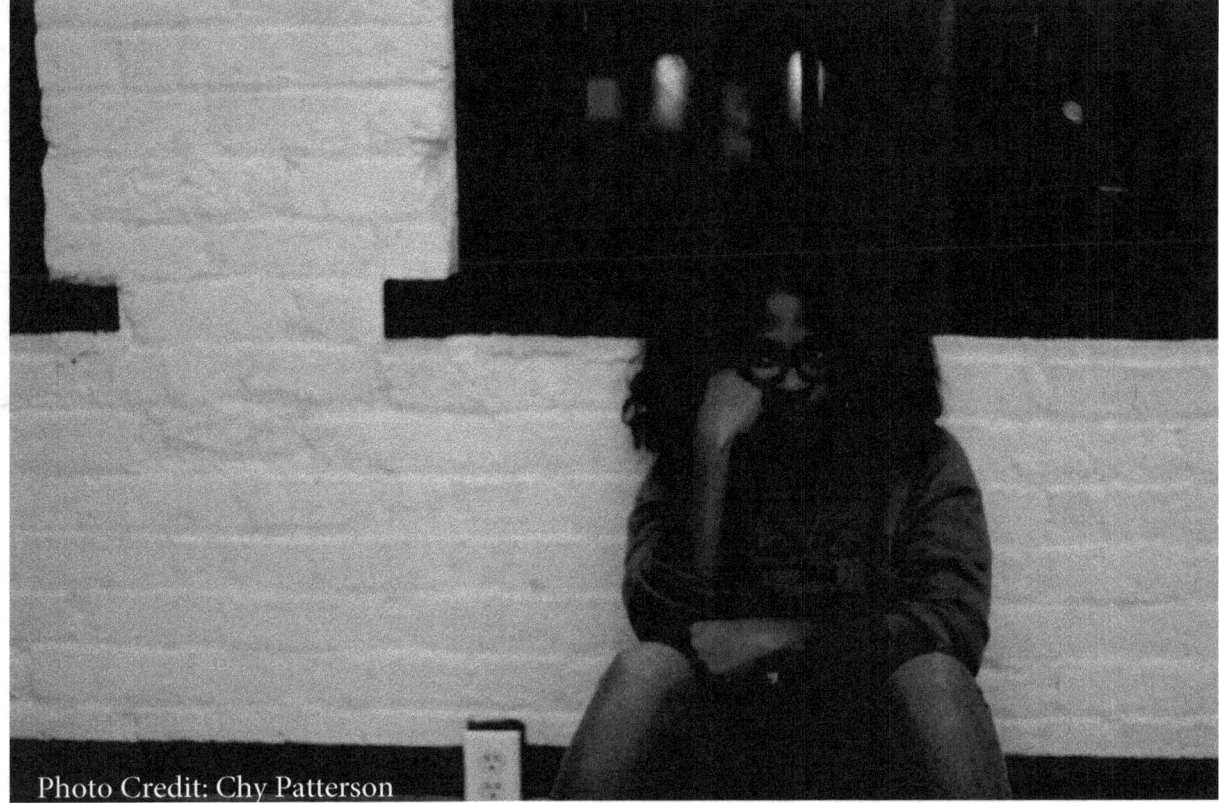

When you win
I win
We all win

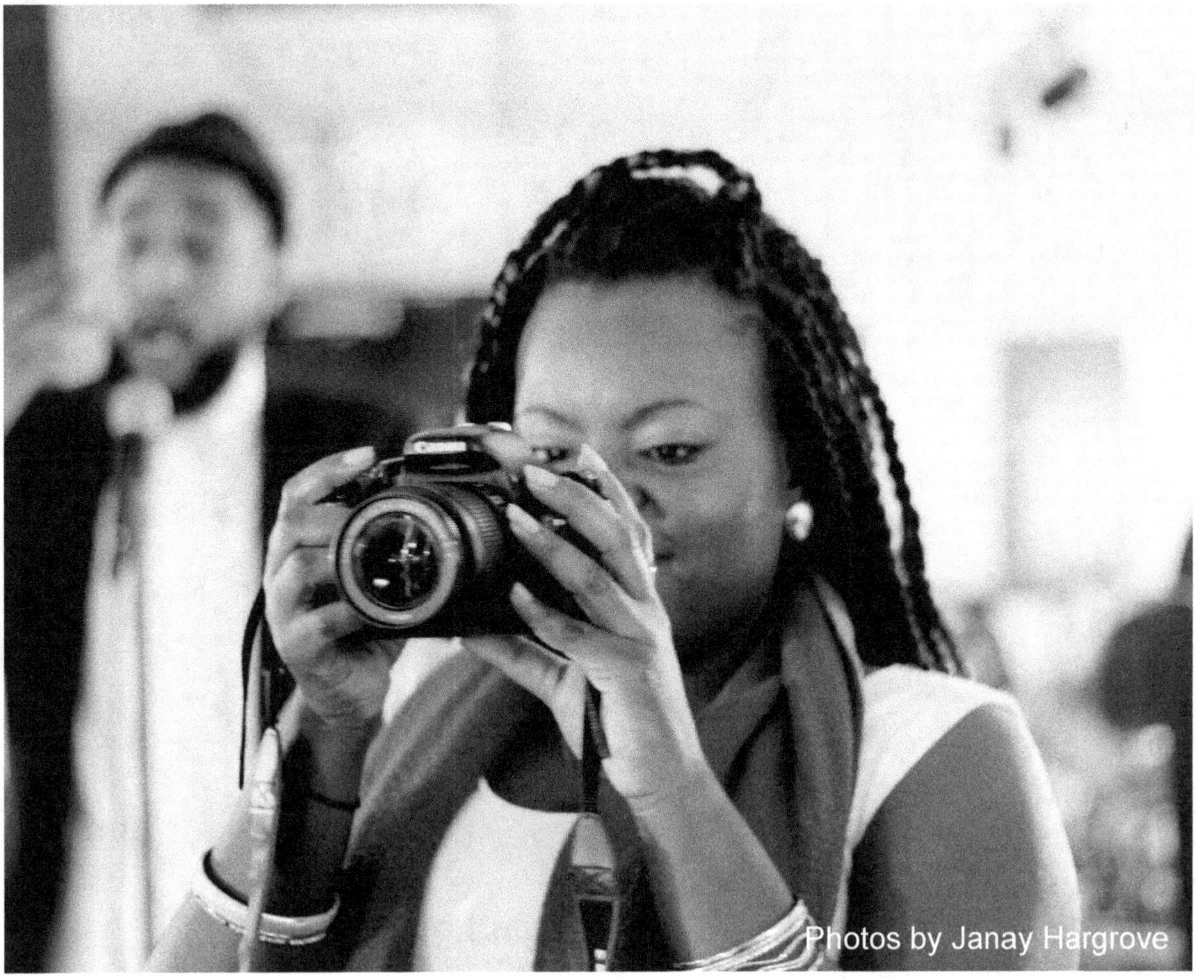

Photos by Janay Hargrove

Jill of
all trades

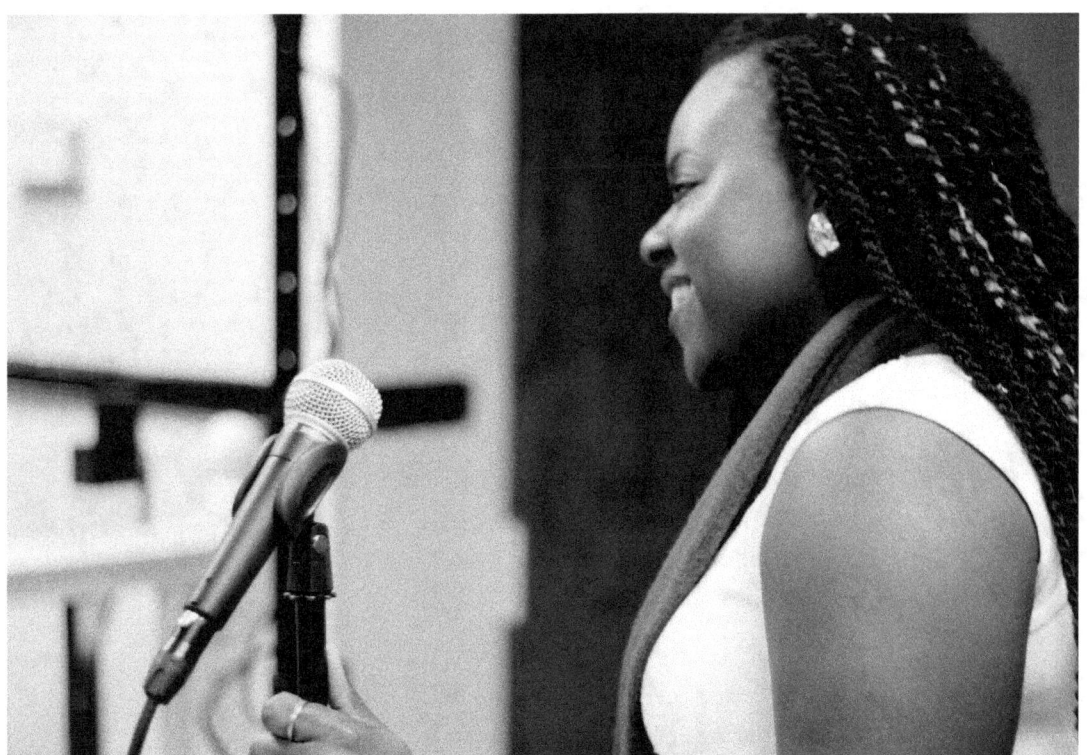

Thank you for your patience.
Your want to be more than what you see.
Your inner diva.
Your calm collectiveness.
Your ability to exude light in layers of black, white and grey.
Your courage, your fear, your authenticity.

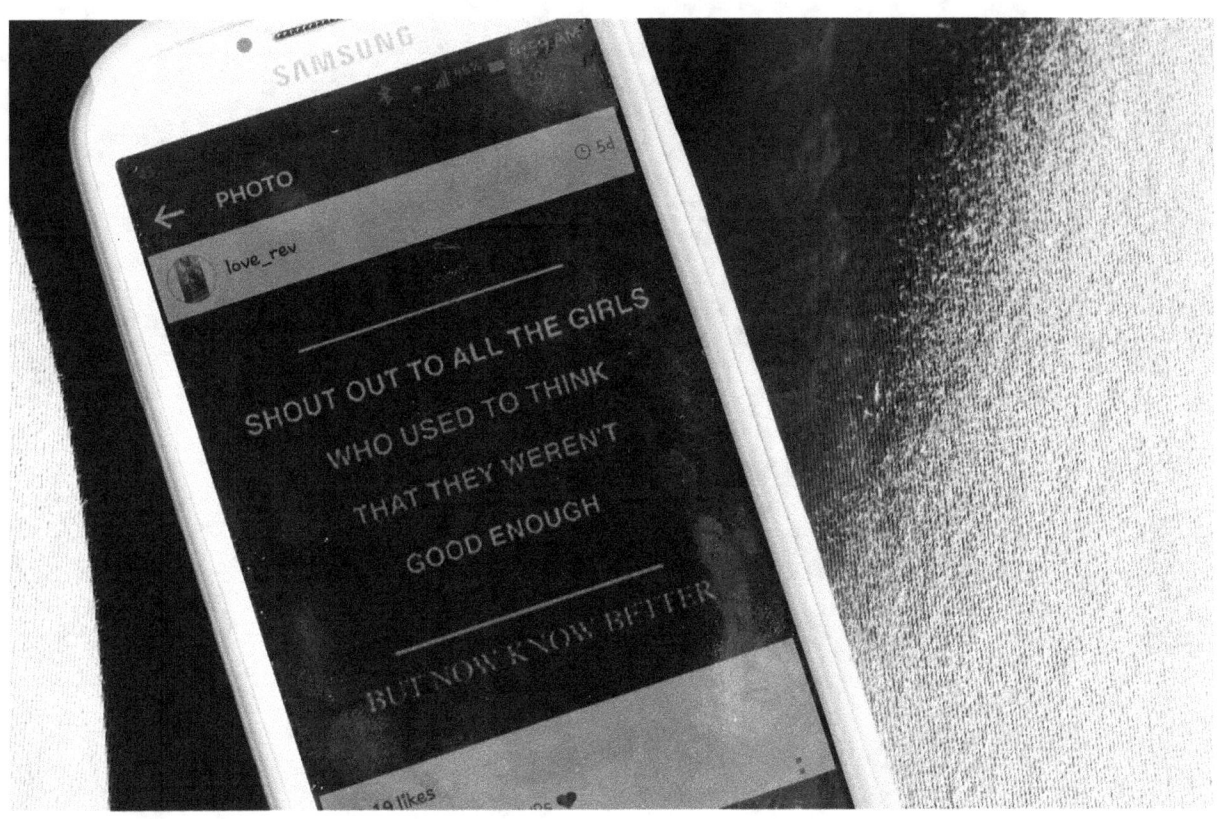